PRIMARY TEACHER'S HANDBOOK

A GUIDE TO SUPPLY TEACHING

MARY ROSE SELMAN
MARY BAIRD

OLIVER & BOYD

Oliver & Boyd
Longman House
Burnt Mill
Harlow
Essex CM20 2JE

An Imprint of Longman Group UK Ltd

First published 1986
Seventh impression 1991

ISBN 0 05 003985 7

Set in Linotron Times Roman 10/12 pt

Produced by Longman Group (FE) Limited
Printed in Hong Kong

ACKNOWLEDGMENTS

The authors and publishers are grateful to the following for permission to
quote the poems and extracts noted:

George Allen & Unwin Ltd for the extract from J. R. R. Tolkien: *The
Hobbit*; Associated Book Publishers (U.K.) Ltd for 'The King's Breakfast'
from A. A. Milne: *When We Were Very Young* (published by Methuen
Children's Books); Blackie & Son Ltd for 'A Spike of Green' by Barbara
Baker; William Heinemann Ltd for 'Acorn Bill' from Ruth Ainsworth: *All
Different*; David Higham Associates Ltd for 'There Are Big Waves' by Eleanor
Farjeon; Penguin Books Ltd for 'Supply Teacher' from Allan Ahlberg: *Please
Mrs Butler* (Kestrel Books 1983) Copyright © 1983 by Allan Ahlberg; Hilda
Rostron for 'Following the Music'; Souvenir Press Ltd for the extract from
Alexander McKee: *How We Found the Mary Rose*.

While every effort has been made to trace copyright owners and sources we
apologise for any omissions in the above list.

Illustrated by Jane Kochnewitz

FOREWORD

This is a book written for supply teachers by supply teachers. Between us, we have been supply teaching for a number of years in many different schools. On talking to head teachers we have found that the approach to supply teaching varies enormously. Of course it is very difficult, given an hour's notice, to leap into your car or catch a bus and then face a class of thirty or more children whom you have never seen before and whose names you don't know. Perhaps you have never worked in that school before or met any of the staff. This book is intended to help you over those first encounters when everyone else looks as though they know exactly what they are doing and you are left to get on with it on your own. Then keep the book beside you and use the ideas as developing themes. Indeed it can be used as a handy source of ideas by most Primary School teachers.

When the telephone rings at 8 am, how many of us immediately think 'Help! What can I do with them today?' We have given you ideas under twenty subject headings – each sub-divided into sections for infant, lower and upper junior work. Although the work is graded to these levels, many teachers will realise that children's abilities differ from school to school and indeed from class to class. Some of the infant ideas can be upgraded to suit lower junior level and in the same way some upper junior ideas can be made sufficiently simple for lower juniors. We don't ask you to follow our ideas to the letter, but to use them, along with your own experience, to fill in those gaps in the day when inspiration runs low. They can often be starting points from which more ideas and work will flow. In order to avoid tedious repetition, we have consciously omitted parts of lessons which we would regard as routine, such as the setting out of materials for art and craft, or the limber-up/warm-up exercises which should precede all PE activities.

Some suggestions will take longer than one session and can be used when supply cover extends over two or three days. They are not intended to be long-term projects. The Quickie pages at the end of each section are not graded but may help while other work is being finished and for those times when there is an odd five minutes to fill.

The Mastercopy pages for each topic are for the duplication of individual copies for the children to use. Many teachers prefer supply teachers to work independently of class exercise books. The worksheets in this book are photocopiable, so that you can make the required number of copies.

Most of the ideas here have been tried and tested by us in various schools, so they do work! Some depend on specific materials being available but we have tried to keep these to a minimum as it is often difficult to find things in a school that you have never visited before. We have included a list of what we consider is a supply teacher's necessary basic equipment store.

It is a good idea to visit any school when you ask to be considered for supply work there. At least you have an idea of the geography of the place and whether working in that situation would suit you. As you return to the school more often, supply teaching becomes easier. The children get to know your face – or you can be sure that one child will point you out as 'that teacher I had the other day'! You know the staff and your way about the school – where the vital stocks are kept and where coffee is served at break time!

The secret of enjoying supply teaching must be in being organised, enthusiastic and confident in what you are doing. Remember to capitalise on your novelty value and to tell the children that your way of doing things will be different from normal. Always introduce yourself clearly to the class and where possible explain the teacher's absence.

We have found that the greatest assets of a supply teacher are adaptability, flexibility and a sense of humour. Formulate your ideas, make your plans, assemble your material but always be prepared to meet any eventuality and, most of all, enjoy your day in school!

SUPPLY TEACHER

Here is a rule for what to do
Whenever your teacher has the flu,
Or for some other reason takes to her bed
And a different teacher comes instead.

When this visiting teacher hangs up her hat,
Writes the date on the board, does this or that;
Always remember, you must say this:
'*Our* teacher never does that, Miss!'

When you want to change places or wander about,
Or feel like getting the guinea-pig out,
Never forget, the message is this:
'*Our* teacher always lets us, Miss!'

Then, when your teacher returns next day
And complains about the paint or clay,
Remember these words, you just say this:
'That *other* teacher told us to, Miss!'

Allan Ahlberg

BASIC EQUIPMENT

1. **Collect together:**
   storybooks
   blank tapes
   a good pair of scissors
   dice
   a stapler
   paper fasteners

2. **Prepare a set of large cards with:**
   Alphabet (both cases)
   Numbers (1 to 20)
   Action words
   Action pictures

3. **Try to save:**
   a. corks, bottle tops, yoghurt pots, cardboard tubes
   b. pictures of people, food, faces, scenery – these should be large, explicit and colourful
   c. records and tapes that you really like

CONTENTS

1 MYSELF

INFANTS

 Written Work and Language

Theme   To make a concertina book including name, age and address

Materials   Paper, pencils and crayons

Method
1. Ask the children to introduce themselves by giving their name and age. How many brothers and sisters are in the school?
2. Discuss how a family is made up. (Remember that not every child has two parents so include grandparents, aunts, uncles and the family pet!)
3. Make sure the children know their own address – the school register is useful.

 Number

Theme 1   To explore size in relation to themselves

Important words   short, shorter, tall, taller

Method   Within the group find out who is the tallest and shortest using different measures – hands and books, as well as rules and tape measures. Ask the children to find something taller or shorter than themselves. Record with pictures.

Theme 2   To make a block graph for eye and hair colour, right- or left-handedness, boy or girl

Method   Organise working groups so that the children are making graphs, asking questions, compiling answers and filling in graphs.

Theme 3   Counting in twos and fours

Method   Use hands and feet to show the children how to make up sums:
a. Count all the girls' hands and feet.
b. Count all the boys' hands and feet.
c. Find the total for the class.

 General Studies

Theme   How we grow

Materials   Pictures of babies, toddlers, infants, children, teenagers, adults, old people

Method
1. Show the children the pictures, which are then to be put in order.
2. Look at the differences. Choose one feature e.g. size, skin or hair. Follow the growth patterns through the ages.
3. Ask the children to think of people they know in these categories. Choose one to draw, and put down general details.

 Art and Craft

Theme
1. Self-portrait with paper and paint, or if scraps of material are available make a collage.
2. Make a paper person with the usual number of physical attributes. The activity can be extended to include 'bendy men'. Use concertina folding for arms and legs and fix them to the body with paper fasteners.
3. To make a 'tall' book. The paper needs to be cut into long pieces.

 Physical Education

Theme   To explore the ways in which we can travel

Method

1. Always practise stopping first! Arrange a sound or signal so the children know when to stop and start.
2. Practise walking, change of direction, pathways.
3. Practise running – slow motion is fun.
4. What other ways? Choose a few children to show everyone (hopefully skipping, hopping, sliding).
5. Make up a sequence. Children repeat, then make up their own. Link the two sequences. This can lead to work in twos, threes or fours. Sequences can be highlighted by vocal sounds or body sounds if appropriate.

 Movement and Drama

Theme   Improvisation of a poem

Materials   Poem 'Following the Music' below; some easy music: nursery rhymes, theme tunes, pop music

Method

1. The poem must be read before the children reach the hall and then again before the action takes place.
2. Make sure the children can do all the actions: stamping, wriggling toes, reaching up and down and rocking. This can form the first part of the lesson.
3. Play the music and let them explore.

Following the Music

I stamp my feet and wiggle my toes
And clap my hands as the music goes.
I reach to the sky and touch the ground,
Up and down to the music sound.
I rock to and fro the way the wind blows,
It's fun to go where the music goes.

Hilda Rostron

LOWER JUNIORS

 Written Work and Language

Theme   To emphasise our individuality by our likes and dislikes

Method

1. Ask the children to write down quickly three likes and three dislikes. Read some to the class.
2. Discuss whether these are really true or influenced by latest fashions and opinions. Have the children always held these feelings or not?
3. Get the children to write more fully about their likes and dislikes, perhaps giving more insight into how these feelings came about.

 Number

Theme   Measuring using hands and feet

Important words   span, width, length, height

Method

1. Check that the children know how to make a hand span and measure with it.
2. Check method of measuring with feet.
3. Set objectives e.g.
   Measure with a hand span:
   a. your book length
   b. the height of the table
   c. along the bookcase
   Measure with your feet:
   a. the length of the room
   b. round the table
4. Record and compile the information about the area and themselves.

 General Studies

Theme   To note the individuality of profiles as well as finger-prints

Materials   Black paper, large white paper for mounting, pencils and scissors, ink pad

Method

1. Make sure the children can lean or lie so that profiles including the whole head can be drawn round. Work in pairs.
2. Cut out results, mount on paper. Print fingerprints on white strip and mount underneath the profile.
3. A class activity can be to guess who is who.

Art and Craft

Theme   To take fingerprints and make pictures from them

 Physical Education

Theme   Alternative use of small apparatus

Materials   Benches, mats, balance bars, hoops, beanbags

Method
1. Set up an obstacle course. Every piece of apparatus has a set movement e.g.
    a. bench – sliding
    b. mats – bunny jumps
    c. hoops – hopping into
    d. beanbags – held between knees
    e. balance bars – using hands and feet
2. Two teams play in relay to complete the course. A system of bonus points for initiative or speed can be added.
3. Time the whole team's effort.

 Movement and Drama

Theme   To re-enact a well-known story

Materials   Use 'The Emperor's New Clothes'

Method
1. Organise the children into parts:

The Emperor	The Queen
The Chancellor	The Council
The Tailors	The Crowd
The Little Boy	

2. You read the story or a synopsis of the story and the children act it out.

UPPER JUNIORS

 Written Work and Language

Theme 1   To write a newspaper report of themselves past, present and future

Method   Discuss the children's memories of childhood, important events, humorous situations. What are they doing now at school and at home? What are their hopes and aims for the future? Explain and read a newspaper report to show the style of reported writing.

Theme 2   Discussion and research work

Method   Fingerprints are personal. Arrange for the children to take prints and compare. When are prints taken now? What were fingerprints used for in the past?

Theme 3   Retelling a story

Materials   Use any moral story e.g. 'The Lion and The Gnat', 'The Buckwheat' by Hans Andersen

Method   'I think I am important' or 'Pride comes before a fall' are titles the children could use for their own stories.

 Number

Theme   Budgeting pocket money

Method   Given £1.50 per week pocket money, how do you budget your money to include your hobbies and general expenditure over one month? Some headings may be cinema, comics, sweets, swimming, clubs, records and tapes. (Set prices if necessary.)
1. List what you would like to do.
2. List what you can do.
3. List suggestions for supplementing your income.
4. How much pocket money do you think you need?

General Studies

Theme   Pulse rate and blood pressure

Materials   Clock or watch with second-hand.

Method
1. Get the children to find their pulse; stress using the first two fingers of the hand, not the thumb. Find the pulse rate by timing for a minute and write it down.
2. Notice differences in the class. Choose several children to experiment by standing on and off a chair ten times and then taking their pulse. Several more can get on and off the chair twenty times and see what happens to their pulse rate under these circumstances.

 Art and Craft

Theme 1   'Inside my head' or 'my head and body'

Method   Ask the children to make a 'working' diagram of what they imagine goes on inside themselves.

Theme 2   To design and draw the sort of clothes that the children would like to wear

 Physical Education

Theme   Large apparatus used to highlight balance which is fundamental to all of us

Method
1. Explain and encourage the idea of balance in the floor warm-up.
2. Children can then work on the apparatus, but arrange a signal so that when given with a simple instruction such as 'Backs', the children can use that part of their body to balance on or accentuate the balance.

 Movement and Drama

Theme   To explore: being alone
being one of two
being part of a crowd
spacial awareness by suggestion

Method
1. Give these instructions:
   a. When you are alone that is your space. Mark out your space around, above and below you.
   b. It is closed and dark.
   c. It is opening, getting lighter and warmer.
      Let the children see others work. Start again in pairs. Start very close – give the same instructions. As before but in a group of five. Again as a whole class.
2. This work demands concentration so lighten the atmosphere by asking children to:
   a. Imagine they are alone and mime that they are a famous film or pop star.
   b. Be two people meeting again after a number of years.
   c. Be people getting into a lift which is almost filled to capacity.

QUICKIES

1. *Question Noughts and Crosses*
   Divide the class into two teams who have to answer questions that identify parts of the body.

spine	hip	cranium
elbow	wrist	shoulder
rib	knuckle	ankle

   Then put questions to each team in turn e.g.
   'It's found at the end of your leg'.
   'Where do you hang your satchel?'

2. *Words from words*
   How many words in five minutes from:
   individual
   skeleton

3. *I-Spy*

2 FEET

INFANTS

 Written Work and Language

Theme 1   'My feet can . . .'

Materials   Paper divided into eight sections, pencil, crayons

Method
a. Start with a class discussion on what the children can use their feet for (standing, walking, kicking etc.).
b. Ask them to illustrate eight uses of their feet, one in each section of the paper and write the 'doing' word underneath.

Theme 2   To act out a story

Materials   Story such as *The Elves and the Shoemaker* from Series 606D (Ladybird)

Method   Tell the story to the children and let them act out parts of it.

 Number

Theme   Measuring feet

Materials   Coloured sugar paper (yellow is a good colour for this work), felt pens or thick pencils

Method   If it is possible ask the children to work in pairs. They take off their shoes and draw round each other's feet. They may need help with drawing. Cut out the feet shapes. Collect all the shapes together and assemble a simple wall-size foot size chart.

 General Studies

Theme   Care of the feet

Important words   foot/feet, toe, heel, sole, arch, ball, knuckle, toenail

Method
1. Have a class discussion on how feet need to be looked after. Stress the importance of choosing the right size and style of shoe. Have any of the class had their feet measured in a shoe shop?
2. Draw a large foot shape on the board and see how many parts the children can name.

 Art and Craft

Theme   Foot shapes
1. Using different coloured paper, make up a flower picture from shapes of feet drawn and cut out. If any are left from the Number activity above, these can be used here.
2. Make a collage picture or frieze using the story of *The Elves and the Shoemaker* as a starting point.
3. Make a foot picture by printing with bare foot, trainer, outdoor shoe, wellington boot. Make up some animal feet as well – bird, dog, duck.

 Physical Education

Theme   'What can you do with your feet?'

Method
1. Different balances on one/both feet.
2. How many ways can you move on your feet?
3. Loud and soft. On a given signal from the teacher use feet to stamp or tiptoe, changing mood or direction or both.
4. Move on different parts of the feet – heels, toes, insides and outsides of feet.

 Movement and Drama

Theme   Rocking

Method
1. Let the children stand with feet apart and practise swaying from foot to foot. Introduce bent knees to make a gentle rocking motion. Try on their own and then link hands in small groups. Exaggerate the movement to show how rocking can take them off balance and into motion. Experiment again in small groups working from stillness to motion.

2. Alter the movement experience by changing stance – feet one in front of the other easily apart. Help the children by using words 'push' and 'pull' to encourage a different effort. Make sure the children use all parts of their feet during these activities. If necessary get them to sit down and feel their feet.

LOWER JUNIORS

 Written Work and Language

Theme   Words ending in 'ing'

Method
1. Introduce the structured work by discussing different actions of the feet. Then use these as a grammar exercise to emphasise the change of verb endings when 'ing' is added.
   a.   losing an 'e' – slide/sliding, stride/striding
   b.   doubling the last consonant – run/running, hop/hopping
   c.   simply adding 'ing' – jump/jumping
2. Free writing: 'What my feet like doing'

 Number

Theme   Measuring with feet

Method
1. Choose two children who appear to have different sizes of feet. Ask both children to measure the length and width of the room using a toe-to-heel step measure. Show the difference between measurements (hopefully showing a vast difference with the size of feet used) and discuss why this is not a satisfactory method of measuring.
2. Estimate how many paces are needed to cover various distances. Children should write their estimate first and the actual pace measurement after. See if there is any standard pace among the children. Is this relative to foot size or leg length?

 General Studies

Theme   To study animal feet

Materials   Black's Children's Encyclopaedia is useful for research

Method
1. Point out that animal's feet can be seen to suit their surroundings. This means that animals (mammals) have adapted from walking on the whole sole (badgers, monkeys, man) to some moving on toes without the heel touching (dogs, cats, animals that move at speed) and others walking completely on their toes which have become horny hoofs (horses, cows, giraffes, elephants). All hoofed animals eat plants and belong to the group called ungulates.
2. Ask the children to select animals and put them into the right group. Note the relationship between locomotion, habitat, whether or not predator, size.

 Art and Craft

Theme
1. Collage picture using different coloured and textured paper, card and fabrics made with cut-out shapes of feet.
2. Artwork to show the sort of shoes that the children wear in differing circumstances – rainy weather, sport, pastimes.

 Physical Education

Theme   Locomotive skills

Method   Find as many different locomotive skills as possible to travel between two points – walk, run, creep, glide, slide, roll, spin.
This activity can be used to find ways of moving from one piece of large apparatus to another.

 Movement and Drama

Theme   Stepping and gesturing

Method
1. First let the children find out how using different parts of their feet makes them move in certain ways.
   a.   Tiptoe – light, small steps
   b.   Heels – slow/balanced, speedy/unbalanced
   c.   Whole foot – stamp, spring

2. Using different directions – forward, backwards and sideways – the children begin to move. Suggest 'stillness' as a means of punctuating their movement.
3. Feet can gesture in the same way as any other part of the body. Practise circling, kicking, stamping. Let the children invent gestures using their feet as a starting point.

UPPER JUNIORS

 Written and Language

Theme   Humorous writing – people who depend on feet

Method
1. Start with a class discussion to name as many people who depend on their own or others' feet in their job or profession – footballers, dancers, runners, climbers, milkmen, postmen, chiropodists.
2. Write 'A Day in the Life of. . .' from any one of these people but written as experienced by their feet.
3. Write a story about 'Choosing New Shoes' written from the same viewpoint as above.

 Number

Theme   Solving time problems

Method   Use the diagram (above right) to answer the questions about our early morning walker.

1. How long does Jeremy Walker take to walk from:
   a. Dunton to Melford?   f. Fenton to Grenley?
   b. Melford to Barby?   g. Grenley to Hidale?
   c. Barby to Corton?   h. Hidale to Landor?
   d. Corton to Epley?   i. Landor to Dunton?
   e. Epley to Fenton?

2. How long does it take him to walk:
   a) from Barby to Grenley   b)   from Melford to Fenton
   c) the round trip?

3. If Jeremy walks at an average speed of 3mph, how far is the round trip?

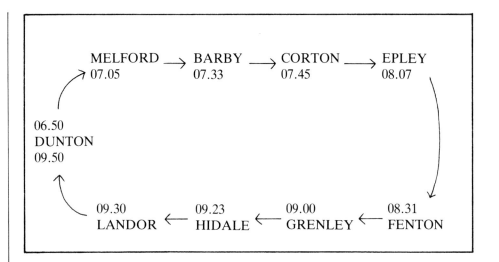

 General Studies

Theme   Footwear through the ages

Materials   Mastercopy 1

Method   The children can choose their favourite design. Ask them to draw comparisons between ages and fashions past and present. Notice that the styles of shoes were much more flamboyant for men in years gone by. Can you give any reason for this?

 Art and Craft

1. The children are asked to design shoes for certain assignments.
   a. to walk on the moon
   b. to go to a disco
   c. to ride a BMX bicycle
   d. for the year 2000
2. 'Choose one of the shoes on Mastercopy 1 and draw it the right size to fit your foot.' Work can be done to explore materials and colours of the shoe.

Physical Education

Theme   Football games

Method
1. Draw a circle on a wall. The players are in pairs and have five goes each to see how many times they can score by kicking the ball into the circle.
2. Teams of six players. The first player kicks the ball onto the wall, the second player must return it to the wall on the rebound and so on down the team. If a player misses the ball or the wall the ball must be passed back to the beginning of the line and the team starts again. If there is not enough wall space for at least two teams to play at the same time, use a watch to time each team's efforts.

 Movement and Drama

Theme   Stylised walks

Method
1. Start with everyone walking naturally, then ask them to march.
2. Now a difference has been established can anyone think of any other type of walk? Suggest parading models, circus performers, processions. Look at different ages – the elderly shuffling, young children tending to bounce as they walk.
3. What about some famous walks – Marx Brothers, John Wayne, Lenny Henry? Usually there will be someone in the class who can perform to order!

QUICKIES

1. How many words can you find that have the prefix *ped-*?

pedestrian	pedal
pedometer	pedicure
pedigree	pedlar
pedestal	pedate
peddle	pedantic

2. In one minute write down all the ways you can move on your feet.

3. Explain the meaning of these phrases or sayings.
   a   Footloose and fancy free
   b. Put one's foot down
   c. Put one's foot in it
   d. Swept off one's feet
   e. Keep one's feet
   f. Best foot foremost

3 EYES

INFANTS

 Written Work and Language

Theme 1   Observation and memory

Materials   Mastercopy 2

Method
1. Look at the sheet for one minute. The children are then to remember and draw as many objects as they can.
2. Go round the class and as each article begins with a different letter of the alphabet, it should be easy to list them on the board and see how many the children have missed.

Theme 2   Memory game

Materials   Tray with ten common objects on it

Method   The children sit round while you show them the tray and perhaps go through the articles with them. Remove one object and see if they can tell you what is missing. The more objects on the tray, the harder the game becomes.

 Number

Theme   Counting in twos

Method
1. Ask the children to look at a partner's eyes and decide what colour they are. Specify the colours at the start – brown, green, grey, blue, black.
2. The children make a line behind each other in their various colour groups. The task is to count the eyes of each group – in twos.

 General Studies

Theme   A look at the eye

Materials   Mastercopy 3

Important Words   Pupil, iris, cornea, lens, eyelash/lid/brow

Method   Look at the eye shape with the children and identify the parts fairly superficially. Do make sure that they can differentiate easily between the eyelash, lid and brow. Stress that that the eyeball rests in a socket. The children can identify the parts of the eye on their own copy and colour the iris and pupil in the correct colours.

 Art and Craft

Theme   Camouflage pictures

Method
1. This work needs a short discussion period before embarking on painting. Choose animals that the children know well to describe the idea of camouflage – giraffe, tiger, zebra, hedgehog. Discuss how these animals can hide in their natural habitat as a protection against enemies.
2. The children can draw their chosen animal and then try to camouflage it by hiding it with the surrounding picture.

 Physical Education

Theme 1   Hoopla

Method   Place hoops on the floor. Arrange the children in teams and get them to throw the beanbag into the hoop from behind a line a suitable distance away. If you give the different coloured beanbags a numerical value, the children can see how many points each team can score.

Theme 2   Greedy lion

Method   Hang a paper carrier on the back of a chair or post. Use scrunched-up newspaper balls to see how many can be thrown into the bag. Each team has a set number of balls and the winners are the ones who get all their balls into the bag in the fastest time.

Theme 3   Hopscotch

Method   If possible mark out a hopscotch pitch in the playground or in the hall if it is allowed.

 Movement and Drama

Theme 1   Follow-my-leader games (These are enjoyed by young children.)

Method   Try to include movements that stretch, curl and involve some different effort actions – slashing, floating, flicking.

Theme 2   Awareness of space

Method   Our eyes help us to see close-up and faraway movements. Different parts of the body can be kept close or can move far away. Let the children experiment with arms, legs, heads, feet, elbows, knees, moving close to the centre of their body and away from it.

Theme 3   To encourage them to be aware of where they are in relation to walls, ceiling and floor.

Method   Allow time for the children to tell you how it feels to keep movements close and small, tight to the body, as opposed to far away, dispersed and free from the body.

LOWER JUNIOR

 Written Work and Language

Theme   Palindromes

Method
1. Explain the word and see how many of the more obvious palindromes the children can think of:- eye, level, madam. Less obvious ones are: pull-up, redder, repaper, reviver, rotator, kayak, put-up, radar, sexes, noon.
2. The children can illustrate the palindromes by finding the pivot letter

and drawing it as a balance. Don't forget Napoleon's famous saying 'Able was I ere I saw Elba'.

3. The children can make up their own palindromes but they must show the pivot letter and it must be able to be pronounced.

 Number

Theme   Venn diagrams

Method
1. Decide on three groups of hair colour – fair, dark and redheads (if you have any in the class). Also pick three groups of eye colours – blue, grey/green and brown/black.
2. On a large sheet of paper prepare the empty Venn diagram as shown below. The children then draw themselves as a small head with the right colour hair and eyes. They have to find the right place to stick their picture on the diagram.

	FAIR HAIR	RED HAIR	DARK HAIR
BLUE EYES			
GREY/ GREEN			
BROWN/ BLACK			

3. To extend this, choose three categories that you notice apply to the children in the class e.g. those with fair hair, those with a red jumper, those with brown shoes. Make a list of the children who fall into each

category and then see if any are in two or perhaps all three. This can then be made into another Venn diagram as shown.

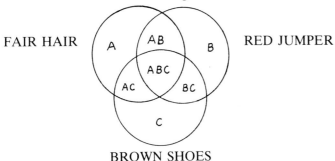

FAIR HAIR   RED JUMPER

BROWN SHOES

 General Studies

Theme   The mechanics of the eye

Materials   Mastercopy 4

Important words   pupil, lens, iris, cornea, retina, optic nerve

Method   Explain to the children that when light from an external object enters the eye the curved surface of the cornea and the lens refract the light and focus it so that points of light from the object produce points of light on the retina. The image thrown is real, upside down and smaller than the object. Light-sensitive cells are stimulated by the light on them and impulses are sent along the optic nerve to the brain, where an impression is formed of the nature, size, colour and distance of the object. The upside-down image is corrected in the brain to show the object as we see it.

    If someone is short-sighted, light from a distant object focuses in front of the retina. If they are long-sighted, light from a close object focuses behind the retina. Short-sightedness can correct itself in old age because the eyeball shrinks bringing the retina further forward.

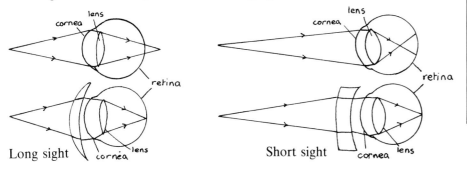

Long sight   Short sight

 Art and Craft

Theme   'My Mum'

Method   Divide a large sheet of paper in two. Draw 'My Mum':
a. As she thinks she looks
b. As she really looks

 Physical Education

Theme   Long jump using distance judgement

Method
1. Divide the class into two teams with a captain each. The captains lay two canes on the floor judging the distance apart by the distance they think the weakest member of their team can jump (obviously the teacher can intervene if she thinks the canes are too close together).
2. Each member of the team jumps, scoring five points if successful and deducting five points if not. The game runs for three rounds but at the start of each round the canes must be placed a hand's width further apart.
3. The game can be made more difficult by asking the children to judge their jumping distance with one eye closed.

 Movement and Drama

Theme   Rising and sinking

Method
1. Let the children stretch as high as they can and sink as low as they can.
2. Alter the time factor – shoot up, sink slowly/rise slowly, sink quickly.
3. Change the direction – rise up in a straight line, sink slowly turning and moving in a large circular movement.
4. Add rhythm to the exercise – pulsate both upward and downward movements. By altering direction and effort a movement sequence can be invented.
5. If the children need more definite images, suggest rockets, fireworks, volcanoes. If they are confident, this sort of work adapts easily to large group involvement.

UPPER JUNIORS

 Written Work and Language

Theme   Use of vocabulary

Materials   Any quotations that make use of the word 'eye' (ref *The Concise Oxford Dictionary of Quotations*)

Method   Can the children explain the meaning and ideas that an author has when writing certain phrases?
1. 'Keep me as the apple of an eye' – *Psalms* xvii.8
2. 'Each turns his face with a ghastly pang
   And cursed me with his eye.' – *The Ancient Mariner* (Coleridge)
3. 'It is easier for a camel to go through the eye of a needle than for a rich man to enter the kingdom of God' – St Matthew
4. 'Beauty is in the eye of the beholder' – Margaret Wolfe Hungerford
5. 'In my mind's eye Horatio' – *Hamlet* (Shakespeare)
6. 'But the Glory of the Garden lies in more than meets the eye' – Kipling
7. 'The worm's eye point of view' – Ernie Pyle

 Number

Theme   The hand can deceive the eye

Materials   A pack of cards

Method   No doubt there will be children in the class who will be willing to demonstrate a card trick. Let's hope that it's not this one!
1. Arrange a suit of cards in this order:- 3, 8, 7, Ace, Queen, 6, 4, 2, Jack, King, 10, 9, 5. Hold the cards face downwards so they cannot be seen. As you spell out A-C-E take one card off the top of the pack for each letter and place it at the bottom. Turn the next card over – it will be the Ace. Put it on the table face upward and leave it there. Continue by spelling out T-W-O in the same way as before. The fourth card you come to will be the two. Leave this face upwards on the table. Continue through the pack, putting a card from the top to the bottom of the pack for each letter you spell out and leaving the named cards on the table.
2. We suggest you have a practice at home before performing in front of the children. It is also possible for the children to be given a suit of

cards to see if they can logically work out the order of the cards for themselves. It will help to tell them to start with thirteen pieces of paper in front of them and then substitute the cards as they work it out.

 General Studies

Theme   Judgement of distance

Materials   Mastercopy 4

Method   For the eyes to focus on a nearby image they must be turned slightly inwards. The eye muscles that control this movement have sensory receptors which respond to the movement. Impulses are sent to the brain to indicate how much the eyes are converging and so give an impression of the distance of an object. Also our stereoscopic vision helps us to judge distance. Try to estimate a distance using only one eye.

Our awareness of objects extends to an angle of 200° although the range of accurate observation is only 2°. To show this, ask the children to try to study more than two letters in any word on the page in detail. More interesting information can be found about an animal's field of vision and judgement of distance.

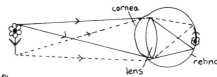

 Art and Craft

Theme   Observation of detail

Method 1   Look at pictures of people of different nationalities and notice the variation in their eye shapes. Using pictures, cut out just the eyes and then draw the face to suit the eyes.

Method 2   Use still life for pure observation drawing.

Method 3   If it is possible to obtain a microscope, use it to study in detail and then draw something you would not normally study so closely e.g. a hair, a piece of skin, a drop of blood.

Physical Education

Theme   'Roll or throw'

Method   Put the children in two teams and number each team 1, 2, 1, 2 all the way down the line. Put the two teams so they are facing one another as in the diagram. Give a ball each to the first 1 and the first 2 in each team. The 1s must throw the ball to each other and the 2s must roll it to each other. Then reverse order back to the beginning again. Penalties are incurred if the ball is dropped. The more space between the children, the harder the game becomes.

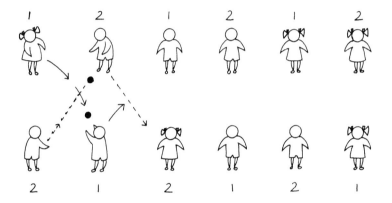

 Movement and Drama

Theme   Winking Murder

Method   The children sit round in a circle. Playing cards are dealt out to each child and these must include one Queen and one Jack. If no cards are available, use blank pieces of paper with two extra marked Q and J. The child who is dealt the Queen is the Detective and declares himself when all the cards are dealt. The child who is dealt the Jack is the murderer and he must keep quiet as it is the detective's job to find him out. The murderer 'kills' his victims by winking at them. Those 'killed' must fall 'dead' on the floor. The game ends when the detective identifies the murderer correctly.

QUICKIES

1. *I-Spy*
2. How many 'eye' songs can you think of in two minutes.
3. Explain these expressions:-
   in the twinkling of an eye
   keep one's eyes on
   see eye to eye
   in the mind's eye
   make eyes at
   eyesore
   eye teeth
   eye of the storm
   eyes bigger than one's stomach.

4 SENSES

INFANTS

 Written Work and Language

Theme   The five senses

Method   Draw a pin man on the board, point to and mark his ears, eyes, tongue, nose, hands and feet. Ask the children what the man does with each part – leading to 'He hears with his ears'. This can be extended to themselves so the final result is 'I hear with my ears'. The children then illustrate each of the five functions literally.

 Number

Theme   Practical reinforcement of numbers 2 and 3 (or any larger numbers at the teacher's discretion).

Method
1. The teacher taps, claps or clicks a number pattern. Choose a child who must reply with the same pattern.
2. When the children are used to following a pattern from the teacher, turn the activity into a circle game where the children pass the number pattern on from one to another.
3. The game can be extended by letting the children find other parts of their body to sound the number pattern.

 General Studies

Theme   Sight

Method   Blindfold one child and ask him to identify another child by touching just his head. Set a time limit and make sure that nobody speaks during the set time.

 Art and Craft

Theme   Taste

Materials   Pictures of as many kinds of food as possible and Mastercopy 5

Method
1. Ask the children to cut out pictures of their favourite foods.
2. Prepare two large pictures for the wall – one showing a crocodile with good teeth and the other showing one with bad teeth.

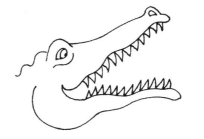 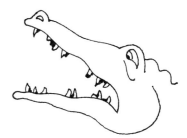

The children must sort out which mouth their food should be stuck into:
e.g.   apples for good teeth
sticky buns for bad teeth

 Physical Education

Theme   Basket of balls

Method   Place a basket full of different sizes of balls in the middle of the playing area. As the teacher empties the basket by throwing the balls about, the children have to catch or collect them and return them to the basket, trying to ensure that the basket is never empty. The game can be extended by the teacher's running and dodging while throwing the balls. Encourage the children to watch the thrower and place themselves where they are likely to catch a ball.

Movement and Drama

Theme 1   To provoke different feelings shown in movement

Materials   A tape made up from any kinds of music in short snatches

Method   It is easier to stipulate beforehand that quick music means sharp, spikey movements, loud music means expansive gestures, quiet music means slow, gentle movements etc.

Theme 2   Sequencing – 'Listen to me!'

Method   Give the children instructions such as 'choose a partner' – 'separate' – 'look for partner' – 'move to partner' – 'touch partner'. Get the children to emphasise which sense they are using as they move. The final sequence can be made up from three or four distinct movements.

Theme 3   Tracking by following a scent

Method   Use the poem below to play a tracking game or just as a simple mime.

> I followed a scent along the ground
> It was a funny smell,
> Was it bad or was it good?
> I thought I knew it well.
>
> Was it sweet or was it sour?
> So difficult to tell,
> I'm sure I've smelt that smell before,
> I'm sure I know it well.
>
> I follow it through the garden,
> Very careful steps I'm taking,
> Through the door, across the hall,
> I know! – It's Mummy baking!
>
> *M.B.*

LOWER JUNIORS

 Written Work and Language

Theme   Creative writing

Method   Take the title 'The Everlasting Sweet'.
1. Is it as good as it sounds? What are the problems – at mealtimes, at bedtime, in class?
2. After a discussion on these disadvantages of what seems like a great idea, ask the children to write their own story. Suggest that it is open-ended but that the time span covered by the story is limited to 24 hours. If not you may find the story as everlasting as the title. Can there be a solution to the problem?

 Number

Theme   Census-taking and percentage work

Materials   Mastercopies 5 and 6 and willing opinion givers

Method
1. Use Mastercopy 5 to take a census of preferences in taste. Depending on the size of the class the sample taken should not exceed fifty opinions. By counting the ticks for each person, they can then be marked down as having a sweet or sour preference.
2. If the final information is doubled it can be transferred onto a hundred square on Mastercopy 6 to show the percentage preference.

 General Studies

Theme   Animal sense of smell

Method   Give the children the headings: Tracking, Rescue, Hunting and Sniffing Out. How do animals help us in these areas by using their sense of smell?

 Art and Craft

Theme 1   To see how and when we need to use perspective when drawing scenes or objects

Materials   Magnifying glass, binoculars, telescope if possible

Method   Using any magnifying aid, let the children choose an object and draw it first as seen close to and then as seen from a distance.

Theme 2   To illustrate the feelings of music

Materials   The tape as suggested in the Infant section for Movement and Drama on page 20

Method   Decide on some circular and linear writing patterns and let the children illustrate the music with these patterns in thick, bold colours.

 Physical Education

Theme   Obstacle courses

Method
1. Set up an obstacle course in the hall or classroom. The children must attempt it blindfolded. The first time they are allowed to study the course before being blindfolded but after that rearrange the course slightly when the blindfold is on.
2. Divide the class into four teams. Two teams play and the other two form the obstacle course. Each team is in pairs – one child sighted and the other blindfolded. The blindfolded child is guided through the course with his partner giving spoken directions. On the second run the partners change over. This can be made into a relay by using more starting points.

 Movement and Drama

Theme   Directed movement sequence using sound and sight

Method   Teacher leads by clapping a rhythm which the children imitate. Then do this while walking. Then blend together clapping and walking rhythms. Ask the children to invent their own sequence.

UPPER JUNIORS

 Written Work and Language

Theme   Interview technique and language development

Method
1. Give the children three minutes to decide which of the five senses they could do without. Let them make notes on their reasons, the problems and possible outcomes.
2. Divide them into pairs and set up an interview situation. Perhaps suggest the form the interview could take.
   'Mr/Miss Smith, I understand you have lost your sense of . . .?' – 'How did this happen?' – 'What problems does it present?' – 'Has it radically altered your life?' – 'How have you learnt to overcome it?'

 Number

Theme   Percentages

Method
1. Decide on a topic for a class survey:
   Favourite pop group
   Television programme
   Food, pets etc.
   Choose five from each category and colour code them.
2. Supposing 25 children in the class, each child has a list of five to choose from, makes his own selection and then asks three more children for their preference. This can be done in the playground or at lunchtime and the information collated in the afternoon.

3. When the results are finalised, the colour codes can be used to show the percentages on the hundred square Mastercopy 6.

 General Studies

Theme   Braille language

Method
1. Use the illustration to ask the children if they can see any pattern in the formation of the letters. You will notice that the sequence runs along the first ten letters, then the second ten, then the last five excluding the letter 'W'. This was not included because the original Braille was written in French and the French did not use the letter 'W'.
2. Ask the children to write their name in Braille using squared paper as a guide. Can they write a question to a friend and receive a correct answer?

A	B	C	D	E	F	G	H	I
J	K	L	M	N	O	P	Q	R
S	T	U	V	W	X	Y	Z	

 Art and Craft

Theme   To fill in the missing half of a picture

Materials   Magazine pictures

Method   Using suitable illustrations from a magazine such as a car, a cake, or a person, cut out the picture in a square or rectangular shape. Place it on the paper and mark the edges so that you can outline the shape. Cut the picture in half and mount either the right or left half in its position inside this frame. Complete the picture by drawing in the missing half.

22

 Physical Education

Theme   Chain ball

Method   Two thirds of the class form a circle, the other third forming a chain inside the circle holding onto each other's waists. A netball is thrown from the circle aimed to touch the last person in the chain below the knee. The one who is touched joins the circle and the one who threw the ball goes to the head of the chain.

 Movement and Drama

Theme   Crowd situations

Method
1. Explain that although individual sounds are easily discernible as words, in crowd situations they are not. What comes over is a 'mood' made by the accumulation of sound.
2. Form groups of about ten children – two groups working while the third group forms the audience. Give directions to show the changing mood of the crowd:-
    whispering – grumbling – chatty party sounds – friendly crowd – hostile crowd
3. Using the above as an example, provide the stimulus by introducing action/reaction. A crowd is established – add an extra person who has previously decided the mood he wishes the crowd to adopt. Let the other children see if he can alter the mood of the crowd.

QUICKIES

1. *Guess who I am?*
   Use riddle-like descriptions of ordinary objects. The children have to guess what is being described.
       'I have one eye and am long and thin. What am I?'
       'I have two hands and a face. What am I?'
2. *Old Macdonald had a Farm* using animal noises wherever possible.
3. Use Mastercopy 2. Put the objects in alphabetical order.
4. *Chinese Whispers* (see also on page 91)
   A message has to be passed all the way around a circle by being whispered from one to another. The message at the end can often bear little resemblance to the original.

5 HATS

INFANTS

 Written Work and Language

Theme   Matching

Materials   Mastercopy 7

Method   The children have to match the correct hat to the correct person. They can colour the pictures and write about them if possible.

 Number

Theme   Counting

Materials   Mastercopy 8

Method   Use the Mastercopy as a game of 'Let's Count':
1. Hats with brims
2. Hats with crowns
3. Hats for men
4. Hats for women

 General Studies

Theme   Hats for seasons

Method
1. Talk about and draw the hats the children wear in the different seasons:
   a.   for rain – Spring
   b.   for sun – Summer
   c.   for wind – Autumn
   d.   for cold – Winter
Ask the children why they need different hats and do they know the different materials from which the hats are made? This activity can

reinforce the learning of the names of the seasons and their proper rotation.
2. Make a large picture for each season and draw people wearing the appropriate hats.

 Art and Craft

Theme   Create a hat

Method
1. Ask the children to draw their favourite hat.
2. Draw a hat for a special occasion.
3. Make a hat from a circle (Chinese coolie). Cut out a large circle of sugar paper. Cut in to the centre once. Slide the cut edges to overlap and stick them together. Decorate the hat and if possible attach some elastic or string to fasten the hat under the chin.

 Physical Education

Theme   Hats on heads

Method
1. Divide the class into four equal teams. Each team has a different colour beanbag – this is its 'hat'. The teams line up the members of each team one behind the other.
2. The team leaders put the beanbags on their heads and on the signal to start walk all the way round their team and back to their place. If the beanbag falls off, they must start again. When they are back in their place, each puts the beanbag on the head of the player behind who again walks all round the team and back to his or her place. This goes on until the last members of the teams are back in their places with the beanbags on their heads.

 Movement and Drama

Theme   Mime

Materials   The song 'My Hat it has Three Corners'

Method

1. Teach the children this song and the mimed actions:

   My hat (*point to head*) it has three (*raise three fingers*) corners (*raise bent elbow in air*)
   Three corners has my hat,
   And had it not three corners
   It would not be (*shake head*) my hat.

2. Play '*Guess the hat*'. Remembering all the hats talked about in the other sections, whisper the name of a hat to each child and tell them to do a short mime for the rest of the class so that they can guess what sort of hat the child might be wearing. The mime could show the sort of job the person who is wearing the hat might do.

LOWER JUNIORS

 Written Work and Language

Theme   Categorising

Method

1. Give the children three headings:- Useful, Ornamental, Professional. Ask them to write a list of all the hats they can think of that fit those descriptions. When they have exhausted their ideas (set a time limit), compare notes and write a comprehensive list under each heading.
2. Ask the children to write a description of a person who would wear a hat in each of the categories.

 Number

Theme   Venn diagrams (see also pages 15 and 16)

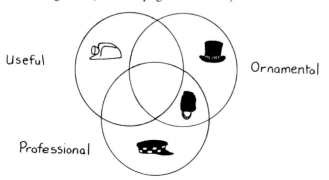

Method   Using the information from the categories in the last section, the children should draw a Venn diagram of hats. If possible they could draw the hats instead of writing the names. Some hats could fall into more than one category e.g. a busby is ornamental as well as professional.

 General Studies

Theme   Hats from other countries

Materials   Mastercopy 8

Method   See how many hats the children can match correctly. Find out if there are any special reasons for some of the hats being as they are (practical use, national costume, religion).

 Art and Craft

Theme   To design a hat

Method

1. Practise making hats from folded newspaper. See if the children can change the appearance of the hat by personal inventiveness.
2. Design a spaceman's helmet making sure that he has all the necessary equipment – some way of seeing, some way of hearing, some way of communicating, some way of eating.

 Physical Education

Theme   'Look, no hands!'

Method

1. Two teams stand in line facing each other. The children must keep their hands on their heads. They have to pass unlikely objects along the line as best they can e.g. beanbags, rubber rings, books, rulers, balloon or ball.
2. Try using small apparatus while the children keep their hands on their heads:- beams, benches, mats, stools. See if the children can adjust their balance to accommodate the lack of hands.

Movement and Drama

Theme   Hat forfeits

Materials   A variety of hats, 2 or 3 beanbags, songs like 'Where did you get that hat' and 'My Hat it has Three Corners' (see Infant section on page 24)

Method   The children sit in a circle with the hats in the middle. The beanbags must be passed round the circle while the song is being sung. The teacher can give a signal for the song to stop and whoever is left holding the beanbag at that point must choose a hat from the centre. Then he must either say or sing something or do a mime in keeping with the hat. Let the class judge the performance. No saying, song or mime can be repeated.

UPPER JUNIORS

 Written Work and Language

Theme   Professional hats

Method
1. Ask the children if they can jot down a list of people who need to wear a hat to do their job. Compile a class list from the individual ones and decide why these people have to wear hats – identity, safety, cleanliness.
2. Written work can stem from any of this and be extended by asking the children to vote for their 'top ten' professions judging by the hats that are worn.

 Number

Theme   Angles

Materials   Protractors. Mastercopy 9

Method   Work out the missing angles from the hats on the sheet.

 General Studies

Theme   Hats through the ages

Materials   Any history books that are available

Method   Up until World War 2 everybody would possess at least one hat. Hats were always worn outdoors. Hats denoted class and style.
1. From the wearing of hats came various phrases and sayings. The class should find out and explain the meaning of these:

   a. to doff one's hat   b. bad hat   c. eat one's hat
   d. pass the hat   e. tit for tat   f. hang your hat

2. Can the children think of or find any more?

 Art and Craft

Theme   Hats with a difference

Method
1. *Hat Consequences*   Use the Mastercopy 9 as a starting point for each consequence. These should provide some amusing pictures at the end.
2. Recreate a hat from a different part of history.
3. 'Cheer up a bowler'. Make a bowler hat template so that everyone starts with the same shape and size bowler. The children should give their hat a character. Do they have someone special in mind to wear it?

 Physical Education

Theme   Throw the hat

Method   Divide the class into two teams (four teams if you are dealing with large numbers). Seat the teams alternately in a circle with a waste-paper basket in the middle. Pass several beanbags (hats) round the circle. At a given signal the passing stops and whoever has the beanbag throws it into the basket. Each successful throw earns a point for the team. Play this game with speed.

Movement and Drama

Theme   'Hats give us a character'

Materials   Box or bag of hats

Method   Let the children choose from the hats and experiment with speech and movement. Try not to put restrictions on them. Devise a way to get pairs of 'hats' to have a conversation. This tends to work better if the teacher takes an active part.

QUICKIES

1. Put the 'hat' into these letters and then explain the word
    ___chet
    ___ter
    t___ch
    c___ter
2. How many names of hats can you give in three minutes? (bowler, trilby, beret etc.)
3. What hats do you associate with the following people?
    The Mad Hatter   John Wayne
    Admiral Nelson   Fred Astaire
    The Pope   Eddie Waring
    Captain Mark Phillips   Russian leaders
    If you can't name them, draw them!

6 CREATURES

INFANTS

 Written Work and Language

Theme   Invention

Method
1. Discuss with the children 'What do you need help with?'
   e.g. scoring goals – to help with that you would need a creature that had lots of legs
   washing up – you would need a creature with lots of hands
   counting – you would need a creature with lots of fingers and toes
2. Ask the children to draw their own helpful creature. They must decide first which task it is going to help them with.

 Number

Theme   Shape recognition

Materials   Mastercopy 10

Method   Ask the children to colour each shape a specific colour: circles – red, triangles – blue etc.

 General Studies

Theme   Small creatures

Materials   Mastercopy 11; book such as *Insects* by A. Wootton
(*A First Look Book*)

Method   How often do we look at really small creatures? Some creatures are insects (six legs). Other creatures have different features (note legs particularly). Use the Mastercopy to count the legs or pairs of legs of each creature. Ask the children where they might see them. How do they feel about them?

 Art and Craft

Theme   To make creatures from random shapes

Method
1. Blot butterfly pictures. Sprinkle or paint with different colour paints onto half the sheet of paper. While the paint is wet, fold the other half over and press down all over. Sugar paper is good for this activity because it absorbs the paint to make a good blot. Cut half a butterfly shape from the folded paper which, when opened out, will give you a butterfly with symmetrical colouring.

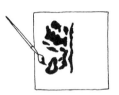 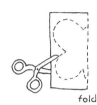

fold

2. Blot creature pictures. The same painting technique is used but then let the children cut their own creature shape from the folded paper.
3. Cut a random shape from black paper for each child and mount it on white paper. The child can then convert its shape into the body of a creature by adding any appendages he or she wishes.

 Physical Education

Theme   Races

Method
1. *Three-legged races*   Make a course for the children so that they have to go out round a chair and then back to the starting point.
2. *Team races*   The team stand one behind the other, legs astride. They have to pass a large ball, balloon or beanbag along the team. It must be passed between the legs from hand to hand.

 Movement and Drama

Theme   Using poems or songs to imitate the movements of creatures

Materials   Either 'The Kangaroo Song' from *Apusskidu* (published by A. & C. Black) or the following poem 'Jump or Jiggle'

Jump or Jiggle

Frogs jump
Caterpillars hump

Worms wiggle
Bugs jiggle

Rabbits hop
Horses clop

Snakes slide
Seagulls glide

Mice creep
Deer leap

Puppies bounce
Kittens pounce

Lions stalk
But – I walk.

Evelyn Beyer

LOWER JUNIORS

 Written Work and Language

Theme   Phonic work

Method

1. Start with some basic work on 'c' sound. Show that sometimes it has to be distinguished from 'k' sound. For this work use the hard 'c' sound as in 'cow' not as in 'ceiling'. Make a list of words that the children can suggest starting with 'c'. See if they can distinguish between nouns, verbs and adjectives.
2. Ask them to use the words that have been suggested to write their own tongue-twister. If they practise the 'c' writing pattern

the children can write their own tongue-twister neatly and use the pattern as a border. This work can then be mounted on the wall inside a large letter C.

 Number

Theme   Division

Materials   Two dice. Prepare four sheets of sugar paper fastened together and draw the outline of a large body and three heads on the paper.

Method   By rolling the dice the children are going to determine the number of eyes, ears, mouths, noses, arms, hands, legs and feet that the creature will have.

1. Divide the class into eight groups and assign one part of the body to each group. The children roll both dice and are told that only even totals are acceptable. The total is then divided by two to decide how many of each feature the creature will have.
2. The group then makes its own features and sticks them onto the basic outline.

 General Studies

Theme   Camouflage

Materials   Book such as *Wildlife of the World – Animals of Africa* by Bent Jørgensen (Hodder & Stoughton)

Method

1. Use the chameleon as an example of how some animals have the ability to camouflage themselves. The chameleon's skin contains tiny cells with granules of different colour in them. When the chameleon is sitting in a green bush, the green granules in the cells expand and the creature turns green. Alternatively, if it is among brown branches, the green granules contract and the brown ones expand and it turns brown. The chameleon crawls along slowly because when it is near enough to its prey it can shoot out its long tongue at lightning speed. The tip of the tongue is sticky and catches the victim fast.
2. Ask the children if they know or can find out what other methods creatures use to camouflage themselves.

Art and Craft

Theme 1. To make a 'helpful headband'

Method If there is a junk-box in the classroom use any bits and pieces to make a headband like the ones below.

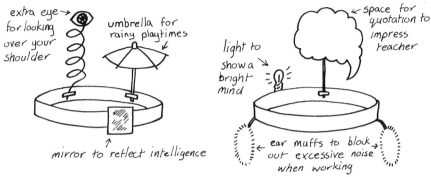

extra eye for looking over your shoulder

umbrella for rainy playtimes

mirror to reflect intelligence

light to show a bright mind

space for quotation to impress teacher

ear muffs to block out excessive noise when working

Theme 2. To make pictures from a template

Method Make a simple fish-shaped template. Use this as a model for the class to make their own. The children draw round the template all over their piece of paper but each shape must touch the ones around it. Use felt-tip pens or crayons to colour the spaces between the fish.

Theme 3. Loo-roll bugs (these take time!)

Materials Cardboard rolls, wool, straws, pipe cleaners, egg-boxes, tissue

Method Wind wool round the cardboard roll. Stick the egg section to the front. Pierce the sides with three pipe cleaners. Stick on straw antennae and tissue-paper wings. Paint after sticking.

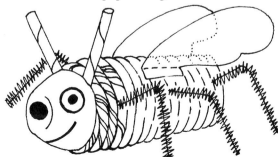

 Physical Education

1. Arrange a circle of floor mats around the room and leave one or two in the middle as a starting point. Give the mats around the outside a creature movement each – crawl, stalk, hop, jump, creep, stride.
2. The children start off on the mats in the middle. On the first signal they choose a mat and move towards it using the creature movement of the mat. When the children have all chosen a mat and are in place on it, give the second signal for the children to move clockwise to the next mat, again using the correct creature movement. On the third signal everyone stops and anyone who is not on a mat is out.
3. After the game has been going for a while and the children are familiar with which mat needs which movement, penalise any child who uses an incorrect movement.

 Movement and Drama

Theme Ritualistic movement

Method
1. Split the class into two groups, with each in a separate circle facing the other. Instil a feeling of tight-knit group security before moving on to the next part of the lesson. If the teacher feels confident then holding hands, arms, waists can be explored by simple movements: walking, skipping.
   a. Get one group to adopt a wide, solid, wall-like stance with feet apart and bent knees.
   b. The other group should be more linear, one foot in front of the other, one shoulder and one arm forward.
2. Keep eye contact between the groups and make a 'showdown'. The children will tend to move in their body shape: the wall-like group, wide, encompassing, spreading round the other group; the linear group with a, piercing, direct, dividing movement. Observe how the children move. Do leaders appear? Which group attacks/defends? Do the children feel comfortable?
3. Change the groups around and impose a framework of rhythm, time, sounds. At first give the children some sound (tambourine, tambour) for movement. As they gain in confidence let them introduce their own sounds.

UPPER JUNIORS

 Written Work and Language

Theme   Dictation

Method   Read aloud the following passage from *The Hobbit*:

'I suppose hobbits need some description nowadays, since they have become rare and shy of the Big People, as they call us. They are (or were) a little people, about half our height, and smaller than the bearded dwarves. Hobbits have no beards. There is little or no magic about them, except the ordinary everyday sort which helps them to disappear quietly and quickly when large stupid folk like you and me come blundering along, making a noise like elephants which they can hear a mile off. They are inclined to be fat in the stomach; they dress in bright colours (chiefly green and yellow); wear no shoes, because their feet grow natural leathery soles and thick warm brown hair like the stuff on their heads (which is curly); have long clever brown fingers, good-natured faces, and laugh deep fruity laughs (especially after dinner, which they have twice a day when they can get it). Now you know enough to go on with.'

J.R.R. Tolkien

 Number

Theme   Fractions

Materials   Mastercopy 6 (100-square)

Method   The idea is to make a creature using the body as one unit (x squares) and the other parts then become a fraction of the whole. The children must be directed that x must be divisible by each denominator of the fractions given below.

e.g. If the body takes 24 squares, the head at $\frac{3}{4}$ is 18 squares, the arms at $\frac{1}{3}$ are 8 squares etc.

The fractions used are:

body – 1 unit, head – $\frac{3}{4}$; arms – $\frac{1}{3}$; legs – $\frac{2}{3}$; eyes – $\frac{1}{6}$; tail – $\frac{1}{4}$; hands and feet – $\frac{1}{8}$.

 General Studies

Theme   Fabulous creatures

Method   Give the children this list of creatures:-   abominable snowman
centaur
phoenix
unicorn

Ask the children to write down anything they know about any of these creatures. At the end of the time allowed, pool all the knowledge and see how complete a profile of each you have between the class. Use library research to fill in any gaps. The children will probably enjoy illustrating their favourite creature.

 Art and Craft

Theme   Imaginary creatures

Method

1. Jot down a description of an imaginary creature. Give the children pencil and paper and ask them to draw the creature as you describe it. They can then colour and decorate their picture.
2. Use curled paper (paper strips rolled round a pencil) to give dimension to the body of any creature. Use the curls either stuck on lengthways or end-on to the paper.
3. Lay down a trace of Marvin glue to form an outline of a creature. Before it dries lay down string to form the eventual shape. If you have any pictures of cave drawings they would be helpful as the children need to aim for simplicity.

 Physical Education

Form the teams as shown in the diagram.

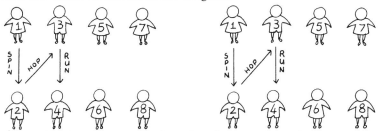

On the signal 1 moves to 2, 2 to 3 and so on along the team. After each move the child sits. Each movement is governed by an instruction from the teacher on how to move e.g. 'spin', 'hop', 'run backwards', 'slide on bottom' etc. The first team to be seated is the winner.

Movement and Drama

Theme   Movement from given stimulus

Materials   The poem below – 'To The Snake'

Method

1. Draw out movement themes from the poem e.g. weight, time sensuousness.
   a. The poem can be interpreted literally by an individual or small group.
   b. The class can explore the movement ideas that arise from the poem – tension, desire, bravado, triumph, a sense of immediacy.
2. Express the poem in abstract whole body movements with the teacher reciting it to give improvisational stimulus.

To The Snake

Green Snake, when I hung you round my neck
and stroked your cold, pulsing throat
    as you hissed to me, glinting
arrowy gold scales, and I felt
    the weight of you on my shoulders,
and the whispering silver of your dryness
    sounded close at my ears —

Green Snake – I swore to my companions that certainly
    you were harmless! But truly
I had no certainty, and no hope, only desiring
    to hold you, for that joy, which left
a long wake of pleasure, as the leaves moved
and you faded into the pattern
of grass and shadows, and I returned
smiling and haunted, to a dark morning.

Denise Levertov

QUICKIES

1. How many words can you make in one minute from CREATURE?
2. Can you complete the following:-

Parents		Young
gander	– goose	
fox	– vixen	
lion	– lioness	
drake	– duck	
buck	– doe	
bull	– cow	
(goat) billy	– nanny	
rooster	– hen	
stallion	– mare	
ram	– ewe	

3. Adjectives describe nouns. Find an adjective to describe each of these creatures:-

   cyclops,   spider,   dragon,   ladybird,   dinosaur,
   shark,   centipede,   serpent,   elephant

7 MYTHS AND LEGENDS

INFANTS

 Written Work and Language

Theme　　Illustrating part of a story

Materials　　'Echo and Narcissus' on page 33

Method　　Tell the story of Echo and Narcissus and ask the children to illustrate their favourite part and write a simple sentence about it.

 Number

Theme　　Pathways

Materials　　Mastercopy 12

Method　　Tell the children to find their way to the centre of the maze.

 General Studies

Theme　　Echoes

Method
1. Ask the children if they have ever been anywhere that they found could make an echo. Explain that sound moves in waves and the ear drum picks up the sound and vibrates, passing the sound message to the nerves in the brain. An echo is produced by the reflection of sound waves from something rigid and approximately vertical.
2. List places that can cause an echo and discuss why others do not (absorption rather than reflection of sound).

 Art and Craft

Theme 1　　To make a narcissus/daffodil type of flower

Materials　　Egg-boxes, yellow paper, glue

Method　　The children cut a six-petal flower shape from the yellow paper, paint a single egg-case yellow and stick it in the centre of the flower. Mount the flower on paper and add a stem and leaves.

Theme 2　　Reflective patterns

Materials　　Letter-writing exercises and thick wax crayons

Method　　See the examples below.

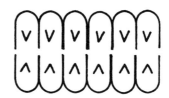 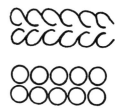

 Physical Education

Theme 1　　Movements over and under apparatus

Method　　Arrange the apparatus so that the children can concentrate on moving over and under. Make a circular arrangement so that they can move clockwise and then reverse the actions anti-clockwise.

Theme 2　　Echo the movement

Method　　Form a large circle. The teacher starts with a simple movement, the next child repeats and adds one of his or her own, third child repeats first two and then one of his or her own. Keep going until a child forgets the movement sequence. Let that child start the game off again.

 Movement and Drama

Theme　　Legs and direction

Method   Get the children warmed up by moving generally round the room. Practise stopping and starting.

1. Legs move you round
   a. Where do they go?
   b. How do they go?
2. Legs can turn you around
   a. on the spot
   b. in the air
   c. along the ground
3. Legs can make shapes
   a. on the ground
   b. in the air
4. Create a simple sequence after the children have explored these movements on their own – travel, turn and jump. This can be repeated three times. Link the work to the story of Echo by asking the children to echo each other's sequences.

Echo and Narcissus

Long ago there was a nymph called Echo who could not stop chattering. She upset so many people that in the end she was punished by never being allowed to speak first, she could only repeat the end of other people's conversations. This punishment was made worse because Echo fell in love with a young man called Narcissus. She wanted to tell him she loved him but when he spoke she could only repeat his words. Narcissus did not understand Echo and repulsed her. Poor Echo, she hid herself away in the caves and mountain cliffs and gradually wasted away until there was nothing left of her but her voice.

Cruel Narcissus, but his cruelty was repaid. One day he came upon a mountain pool which was clear and still, the water gave a perfect reflection. Narcissus, feeling thirsty, bent to drink and saw himself for the first time in the water. He thought it some beautiful water-spirit and tried to touch it, but of course the face disappeared. He stayed gazing at the image and gradually he fell in love with the reflection. He begged the face to come out of the water but each time he reached to touch it, it disappeared. Narcissus could not bear to leave the pool and he too faded away and passed from the upper world. However where Narcissus had knelt for so long there appeared a flower with a dark heart which we know now as the Narcissus.

LOWER JUNIORS

 Written Work and Language

Theme   Recounting a story through writing

Materials   'Theseus and the Minotaur' on page 34

Method   Find out if the children know the difference between a myth and a legend.
Myth – a story which is entirely made up
Legend – a story which has been passed down by word of mouth and is not entirely true
After hearing the story of Theseus, the children may choose to recount their favourite part of the story and illustrate it. This activity can be altered by getting the children to write and illustrate the story in the form of a frieze.

 Number

Theme   String measurement

Materials   String, ruler

Method
1. Make sure the children know the meaning of perimeter and circumference. Show the children how useful string can be in measuring awkward objects. Explain how to use the string for this purpose and select objects in the room to measure as a class. Before the children measure their own choice of objects they must estimate the length. This can be recorded and they can see how near their estimate was to the actual length. The easiest things to measure are around themselves: wrist, head, waist, ankle, finger.
2. This general theme can also be used to teach or revise Roman numerals.

 General Studies

Theme   Legends

Materials   'Theseus and the Minotaur' on page 34

Method
1. Originally the story of Theseus and the Minotaur was thought to be a myth, but in the early 1900's Arthur Evans found the ruins of a palace in Crete. The ruins looked like a maze or labyrinth. When the palace was restored it was beautiful. On the walls were symbols of Zeus and also pictures of a youth somersaulting over a bull while others waited to catch him. This was obviously the source of the story of the Minotaur, but the young people were not given as tributes to the bull, they were trained as acrobats to perform with the bull in ceremonies honouring Zeus.
2. Legends come from many countries. See if the children can find any more legends e.g. Beowulf, King Arthur, Tristram and Isolde.

 Art and Craft

Theme   String patterns

Materials   Four saucers of different colour paint and four lengths of string

Method
1. The piece of paper to be used should be folded in half. Dip the string in the paint and lay it on one half of the paper. Fold the other half on top and as you hold it down with one hand, pull the string out firmly with the other. This should leave a trace pattern behind when the paper is opened. Repeat with different colours.
2. Stick a string pattern on a piece of thick paper or card and use it to print with. If the pattern is small it can be used as a border around another picture.

 Physical Education

Theme   Rolling and tumbling

Method   Use mats individually so that the children can practise certain movements.
1. Rolling – sausage-like, forward roll, backward roll, curled up rolling sideways
2. Circle roll
   a. Sit cross-legged, hands under knees holding feet. Rock sideways until whole body rolls sideways onto shoulders and round to sit up again.

b. The circle roll can also be done sitting with legs straight and apart (hold feet). To get the impetus swing one leg across the other leg and roll backwards with leg circling over head; the body and the other leg follow.
3. Put all the mats together and let the children make up a tumbling sequence. They can include leap-frogging and jumping.

 Movement and Drama

Theme   To recreate the story of Theseus

Materials   'Theseus and the Minotaur' below

Method   Divide the class so everyone has a part to play. You will need Aegeus, Theseus, Ariadne, Minotaur, young people. The rest of the class can make a crowd on the cliff, Theseus' boat and a labyrinth.

Theseus and the Minotaur

Theseus was a young Prince of Athens who went as part of a group of young people sent to Crete as a tribute to be given to the Minotaur, a monster, half man, half bull, who lived in a Labyrinth. His father, King Aegeus, was desperate that Theseus should not go, but Theseus said he was confident that he would slay the Minotaur and return triumphant in a ship with white sails to Athens.

On arriving in Crete, Theseus fell in love with Ariadne, the King of Crete's daughter, and because she loved him she gave him a golden sword with which he could protect himself. Theseus hid the sword, but Ariadne also gave him a ball of string for she knew that once Theseus found himself in the Labyrinth he would not find his way out without help. So Theseus, armed with the sword, went into the Labyrinth and tied the string to the inside of the door and unwound it as he went to find the Minotaur. There was a furious battle when Theseus and the Minotaur met but Theseus eventually won and the monster lay dead. Theseus then rewound the string and gathered all the other young people. Together they made their way to their ship where Ariadne waited. Filled with delight they hurried on board and immediately set sail for home. In their haste they forgot to change the sails of the ship which remained the dismal black of the outward journey.

King Aegeus waited on the cliff hoping for the return of his son. At last he saw a ship approaching but it had black sails. The King was so unhappy that in his grief he threw himself into the sea and drowned.

UPPER JUNIORS

 Written Work and Language

Theme   Modern myths

Materials   'Echo and Narcissus' on page 33 and 'Theseus and the Minotaur' on page 34

Method   Using the information from the Infant and Lower Junior sections on pages 32–34, go into more detail about myths and legends.

1. Explain that to the Greeks whatever had motion seemed to be alive – sea, stars, trees etc. They invented gods who were in their own image, yet immortal. They needed stories to explain the mysteries of evil, growth, death, and fire so myths were invented to explain the unknown. Tell the children the stories of Echo and Narcissus, Theseus or any others you can remember.

2. Myths are not all thousands of years old. Ask the children to think of and try to explain some more modern myths e.g. Father Christmas, Jack Frost.

 Number

Theme 1   String measurement

Materials   Mastercopy 12

Method   Give the children some lengths of string and ask them to find out the distance to the centre of the maze in centimetres.

Theme 2   Time line of civilisation

Materials   The information below (dates are very approximate to make the drawing easier)

Method   The children, either as a class or individually, should draw a time line with the dates in the proper sequential order.

1. Above the line enter the facts about civilisation in Britain.

Stone Age	250,000 BC–2000 BC
Bronze Age	2000 BC–1000 BC
Iron Age	1000 BC–55 BC
Romans in Britain	55 BC–AD 400
Saxons and Vikings	AD 450–AD 1066

2. Below the line enter the facts about world civilisation.

Egyptians	4000 BC–2000 BC
Greeks	2000 BC–300 BC
Romans	300 BC–AD 500

Obviously the line cannot go back anywhere as far as 250,000 BC but if it continues to 2000 AD the children should be able to realise what a small part modern history plays in the history of the world.

 General Studies

Theme   Greek architecture

Method
1. The style of Greek architecture can most easily be seen in the temples they built. The patterns on which they were built were called 'orders'. There are three important ones, best seen in the columns that supported the temples.
   a. Doric – the least ornate, seen in the Parthenon
   b. Ionic – distinguished by large scrolls, a design used later by the Romans
   c. Corinthian – most slender, the capital decorated with acanthus leaves; style seldom used by the Greeks, more by the Romans

2. The temples were for the gods to live in, not for people to worship in. Inside the temple was a statue of a god or goddess but it rarely faced the entrance.
   a. Temples were very dark with no windows. The smell would be of incense burning and flesh from sacrifices.
   b. Temples were originally built from wood – the fluting on the pillars was the easiest way to trim a tree. This design was then transferred to stone.
   c. Stone pillars were not necessarily to support the temple, they were purely decorative.

 Art and Craft

Theme   Mosaics

Method
1. These pictures can be made from small shapes cut from coloured pictures in magazines. Draw a simple outline first and then fill in. Dried, clean, crushed eggshells make a good medium, also dried pasta shapes. Paint these after the mosaic is completed.

2. Greek columns make a good subject for careful drawing but reference pictures are needed (see also page 35).
3. Illustrate an impression of a nymph, dryad, Minotaur or any of the Greek gods.
   a. Zeus – most powerful father – lightning, thunder, rain
   b. Poseidon – lived under the sea – water, earthquakes
   c. Apollo – manly beauty – music, medicine, archery

 Physical Education

Theme   Rolling and tumbling

Method   Use the lesson notes as suggested in the Lower Junior section on page 34 but get the children to master leap-frogging and rolling in a circle as basic skills.

 Movement and Drama

Theme   Music as an aid to drama

Materials   Music of 'The Planets' by Gustav Holst

Method   Use the music as a starting point for dramatic music. Explain that the Romans adopted the Greek gods but gave them different names.

Greek	*Roman*	*Greek*	*Roman*
Zeus	Jupiter	Ares	Mars
Aphrodite	Venus	Hermes	Mercury
Kronos	Saturn	Poseidon	Neptune

QUICKIES

1. From the list on the right can you identify the gods?
a.	Venus	a beautiful youth
b.	Apollo	the god of wine
c.	Mercury	the Titan who stole fire from heaven
d.	Adonis	the goddess of love
e.	Bacchus	god of the sun
f.	Prometheus	a winged messenger

2. Find out the original Seven Wonders of the World and in which country you could find them.

3. See how quickly you can complete the following sums
   1. Add together $\frac{1}{2}$ of 2698 and $\frac{1}{4}$ of 4664
   2. Add 4927 to $\frac{1}{2}$ of 1996
   3. Add together $\frac{1}{3}$ of 783 and $\frac{1}{5}$ of 1020
   4. Find the total of $\frac{1}{8}$ of 1200 and $\frac{3}{4}$ of 124
   5. Helen spent £3.50. Her sister Amy spent only half as much. How much did they spend altogether?
   6. Andrew can jump 2.24 m. James can jump half as far again. How far can James jump?
   7. Dad's petrol tank holds 36 litres but he uses $\frac{3}{4}$ of the petrol to get to work. How much petrol is left in his tank?
   8. Mark cuts the cake into six equal pieces. He eats two pieces for tea. What fraction of the cake is left?

8 SPRING

INFANTS

 Written Work and Language

Theme   Poetry

Materials   The poem 'A Spike of Green' below

Method   Read the poem to the children and if possible reproduce it on a large piece of paper. Talk about the new life that we see in Spring. The children can draw pictures of spring flowers, lambs, birds and of course the spikes of green in the flower-pot.

A Spike of Green

When I went out
The sun was hot,
It shone upon
My flower pot.
And there I saw
A spike of green
That no one else
Had ever seen.
On other days
The things I see
Are mostly old
Except for me.
But this green spike
So new and small
Had never yet
Been seen at all.

Barbara Baker

 Number

Theme

Materials   Symbols drawn on paper, crayons, paper cut to size for a book

 Method   Get the children to find things smaller than themselves and point to things larger than themselves. Expand the discussion to include animals, people and natural things. Show them the symbols for 'larger than' and 'smaller than' and relate them to themselves and the things they have mentioned. Let them choose three larger and three smaller to be drawn on individual pieces of paper. Perhaps the quicker children could write a sentence as well. The pieces of paper can then be put together into their own book.

 General Studies

Theme   Animals and their young

Materials   Pictures of animals

Method   Most animals produce their young in the Spring so this is a good time for some work on the names of animal young. Use large pictures of fully grown animals and see how many young of these animals the children can name. Move on to other animals, birds and fish.

Art and Craft

Theme 1   To make spring flowers

Materials   Tissue paper, silver foil scraps, paper cake cases

Method   Use the cake cases as flowers and decorate them with paint or crayon. Add tissue paper for inner petals. Mount the flowers on pre-drawn stems and leaves.

Theme 2   To make a card with flowers inside

Materials   Piece of A4 paper, cut-out flowers, glue

Method   Fold the paper into quarters to make the card shape. Open the paper out and fold in half lengthways. Make a 1 in (2.5 cm) cut about a quarter of the way along the fold. Bend the cut edge towards the nearest end of the paper. Open the paper out and return it to the card shape. When opened the card should have a triangular piece which sticks out to form a 3D vase. Stick the pre-cut flowers (see above) in the vase.

Physical Education

Theme   Springing, bouncing, jumping

Method   Use the poem 'Jump, Jump, Jump' as a starting point to see how many different ways the children can jump (see below).

Jump, Jump, Jump

Jump – jump – jump
  Jump away
From this town into
  The next, today.

Jump – jump – jump
  Jump over the moon;
Jump all the morning
  And all the noon.

Jump – jump – jump
  Jump all the night;
Won't our mothers
  Be in a fright?

Jump – jump – jump
  Over the sea;
What wonderful wonders
  We shall see.

Jump – jump – jump
  Jump far away;
And all come home
  Some other day.

Kate Greenaway

 Movement and Drama

Theme   Extensions in space, gathering and scattering

Method

1. Work on gesturing with arms (together and singly), reaching for something and bringing it to themselves. Remember levels and speed of action. Extend this to let the children move to reach something. Give the 'thing' a quality (fragile, heavy, hot etc.) and from there enlarge the gestures so that the movements become gathering ones.

2. Once they have 'seen' the object, let them give or throw it away. Note the difference of effort involved. Follow the same sequence of ideas as for gathering.

3. Let the children make up a movement sequence and give it a story of their own.

LOWER JUNIORS

 Written Work and Language

Theme   Homonyms

Method   Explain what homonyms are and give the most obvious one for this time of the year – Spring. Ask the children to give you sentences to show that they appreciate the different ways the word can be used. Tell them to make their own list of homonyms. Here are some starters:- Red/read   there/their   tide/tied   sea/see   made/maid

 Number

Theme   Plotting points

Materials   Squared paper

Method   Perhaps it would help to start with a small shape to remind the children how to draw and number the axes. Remind them that the point where the two lines meet at the bottom left-hand corner is always 0 and that the directions are always given with the horizontal axis first.

1. *The flower* needs a horizontal axis of 10 and a vertical axis of 15. When they have plotted two points, they should be joined together.
    (4,1) (4,4) (6,4) (6,9) (5,9) (6,11)
    (4,9) (4,14) (6,12) (5,14) (8,14)
    (7,12) (9,14) (9,9) (7,11) (8,9)
    (7,9) (7,4) (9,4) (9,1) (4,1)

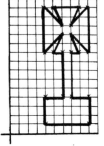

2. *The rooster* needs a horizontal axis of 10 and a vertical axis of 10.

    (1,4) (1,6) (3,8) (5,6) (5,4) (7,4)
    (7,6) (9,7) (10,6) (9,6) (9,4) (8,3)
    (8,0) (7,2) (5,0) (5,1) (3,3) (3,2) (1,4)

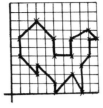

 General Studies

Theme   Spring tides

Method
1. A tide is the flowing or swelling of the sea that happens twice daily due to the attraction of the moon and the sun. A spring tide is a full tide that occurs at the new and full moon, when the attraction of both sun and moon act in a direct line.
2. See if the children can find some more information on tides: the Severn Bore; why the Mediterranean Sea is not tidal. They may also be interested in the movement of the sun and moon around the earth and how it affects our natural conditions.

 Art and Craft

Theme   Cards

Materials   See the pictures below

Method   As Valentine's Day falls in the spring term, here are two designs of cards to make.

Threaded red wool through holes punched in card. Red heart with message in the middle.

Three contrasting shades (pink, purple, red) of tissue paper stapled in the centre. Cover staple with a silver star.

 Physical Education

Theme   Jumping games

Method
1. Long jump using large hoops: space the hoops close together at the start. Jump from one foot to another, from hoop to hoop. Increase the distance between the hoops after each round.
2. Use the same hoops for standing jumps, jumping from both feet to both feet from hoop to hoop. Keep increasing the distance between hoops.

Who can jump the furthest in each category?

 Movement and Drama

Theme   Space words

Important words   Space words:-
    near, far, above, below, around, over, under, through, towards, away

Method   Spring is a time of new growth and energy. Choose a combination of the space words and get the children to work on their interpretation in small groups. They can move together or copy each other, use each other as props or pass the movements from one to another.

UPPER JUNIORS

 Written Work and Language

Theme   Poetry

Materials   The poem 'On a March Morning' on page 40

Method
1. Use the poem and see if the children can create their own poems about a spring morning in school.
2. This poem provides instant material for a frieze.

On a March Morning

A smell of warmth in the air,
A sea of books in the library,
The buzz of conversation,
Shouts of glee from a PE class,
The echo of feet running through the corridors,
The beginnings of bean plants,
A smell of burning,
Sleepy cars resting in the car park,
Tapping of the gardener's hammer,
Dewy grass scattered with daisies like snowflakes,
The remains of an orange scattered round a bin,
The beginnings of a currant pudding . . . .
Fish mobiles hanging from the ceiling,
Faces painted and stuck on the wall,
Mrs Newman is teaching English,
A sea with ships,
'Finishing off' time,
Mrs Sequeire teaching maths,
The beginning of an icy picture,
Mrs Saxon teaching reading,
Pictures of faces and monsters,
Miss Sumpster teaching writing,
Bird mobiles hanging from the ceiling,
Poetry and pictures,
Paper men and women hanging from the wall,
Mr Smith teaching geometry.
Drawing circles and shapes,
And a weasel and a stoat stuffed and on show.

Jacqueline Davis, 10.

 Number

Theme   12-hour and 24-hour clocks

Method   Get the children to draw a conventional 12-hour clock. Draw another circle outside it and add in the hours from 13 to 24. With the aid of this the children should be able to answer the following questions:

1. Change these times into 24-hour clock times
   11.30 am   10.55 pm   2.10 am
   7.45 pm   6.25 pm   10.15 am
2. Change these times to 12-hour clock times
   11.15h   23.00h   16.10h
   17.20h   04.25h   21.45h

3.

London 11.45	Luton 12.30	Kettering 12.55	Leicester 13.15	Nottingham 13.55

Write each of the times as 12-hour clock times. From the timetable find out how long it took the train from London to each of the named places.

 General Studies

Theme   Rubber. Spring is the time when sap rises in the trees to promote new leaf growth. In one particular tree the sap is even more useful.

Method
1. Although synthetic rubber is now produced in great quantities, tell the children a brief history of where the original product came from. They can find out how it was collected and produced.

   – In 1493 Christopher Columbus visited Haiti and found the natives playing games with a 'rubber' ball.
   – A century later the sap from the rubber tree (latex) was being used in Mexico as glue.
   – In 1735 rubber trees were found in the forests of the Amazon in Brazil.
   – Rubber was found subsequently in Africa and Asia.
   – British planted rubber trees in their colonies in Malaysia.

2. Ask the children to list all the things they can think of that might use rubber in their production.

 Art and Craft

Theme 1   Remembering that March may 'come in like a lion and go out like a lamb' construct a paper windmill to blow in the winds.

Method

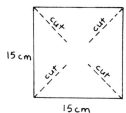 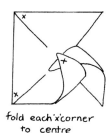 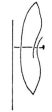

15 cm

15 cm

fold each 'x' corner to centre

attach loosely to cardboard stick with paper fastener

Theme 2   Paper weaving

Method   This can be done in the conventional way with long rectangular strips woven through straight cuts on the paper, but if you vary the cuts on the paper (make them zig-zag or curved) the work can take on a new dimension. Use of colour can be very important.

 Physical Education

Theme   Jumping game

Method   Practise jumping – a quarter turn, a half turn, a full turn to right and left. Give directions for a sequence of movements (running, stepping, rolling) but alter the end or intersperse at a given signal with a jump chosen from the list. Anyone who turns the wrong way or does the wrong jump will be out.

 Movement and Drama

Theme   Extension in space

Method   Spring is a time of growth – elaborate on this simple idea by exploring growing and shrinking movements.
1. Work individually at first, not only using different directions but different levels to start from and finish at. Emphasise movement close to the body and movement away from the body.
2. From this work ask the children to think more carefully about the parts of their bodies that can lead a movement – shoulders, hips, knees, elbows are as important as head, hands and feet.
3. Towards the end of the class time divide the class into groups to work together. Suggest a breathing rhythm as a basis for their interpretation of the themes explored in growing, shrinking, rising and falling.

QUICKIES

1. Which words are incorrectly spelt?
    accomodate
    programe
    misfortune
    beatiful
    wooly
    aquaduct
    inflamation
    houswork

2. Draw a pin man on the board or a piece of paper and call him 'The Sound Man'. Use parts of the body for phonic work e.g.
    'arm' to find other words with 'ar' sound
    'knee' for 'ee' sound
    'foot' for 'oo' sound
    'waist' for 'ai' sound
    'mouth' for 'ou' sound
    'face' for work on the magic 'e'

3. The signs have been left out of the following sums. Can you put them in correctly?
    a. $3 \square 2 = 4 + 1$
    b. $9 - 2 = 6 \square 1$
    c. $2 \square 2 = 5 - 1$
    d. $5 \square 1 = 7 - 1$
    e. $6 \square 3 = 2 \square 1$
    f. $3 \square 10 = 6 \times 5$
    g. $3 \square 1 = 4 \square 2$
    h. $4 - 1 = 2 \square 1$

41

9 SUMMER

INFANTS

 Written Work and Language

Theme To make a simple sentence using as many of the given 's'-sound words as possible

Materials The diagram below

 Number

Theme 1 To count and colour

Materials Mastercopy 13

Theme 2 (For older infants) Number stories

Materials Mastercopy 14

Method Use the line of ten objects to make up sums within the number story of 10.

 General Studies

Theme Drying

Method Have a class discussion on the difference between wet and dry, related to:

1. home experiences: – drying hands, drying washing
2. outside the home: – water evaporates
3. worldwide: – drought

 Art and Craft

Theme 1 Pictures of 'me' dressed for winter contrasted with 'me' dressed for summer

Theme 2 Sand and glue pictures

Method A pattern is drawn with watered-down Marvin, then sand sprinkled on. If no sand is available, detergent powder can be used on black paper.

 Physical Education

Theme Ball skills

Method
1. Make a line of children (perhaps half the class). Pass the ball to the back of the line between legs and back again over heads.
2. Up-end a climbing stool. Use this as a 'goal' for throwing netball.

 Movement and Drama

Theme To dramatise simple songs

Materials
1. The song; 'Row, row, row your boat' below or
2. The song 'The Sun has got his hat on' on page 43

Method 1 Form the children into two equal circles facing each other so that each child is sitting down opposite a partner. On the first two lines of the song the children make a rowing action with their partner. On the last lines they stand up and gallop to the right. At the end of the song they should be opposite a new partner ready to start again.

> Row, row, row your boat
> Gently down the stream,
> Merrily, merrily, merrily, merrily,
> Life is but a dream.

Method 2   Choose three or four children to be 'suns'. The rest stand as statues waiting to be brought to life as the 'suns' skip in between. Or the rest of the class can be seeds in the ground waiting to grow into flowers in the sunshine.

> The Sun has got his hat on,
> Hip, hip, hip hooray,
> The sun has got his hat on
> And he's coming out to play.
> Everyone is happy, everyone is gay,
> The sun has got his hat on and he's coming out to play.

LOWER JUNIORS

 Written Work and Language

Theme   Cloze Procedure. Reading Level 7+

Method   Write the following passage on the blackboard and ask children to fill in the blanks. Sometimes more than one word will fit, so as long as the sense of the passage is kept a different word from the given one is acceptable.

> It ____ summer. Jane and Michael wanted to go ____ a picnic at the beach. They lived ____ the sea. Mother ____ some sandwiches and gave ____ some orange juice to drink. They were going to ride ____ bicycles. "Be careful!" ____ Mother. "Goodbye!" said Jane and Michael. Soon they were ____ the seaside. It was ____ hot. They went for a swim in the ____. Then it was time to have their ____. At 5 o'clock they ____ their bicycles home.'

(was, for, near, made, them, their, said, at, very, sea, tea, rode)

1. What time of year was it?
2. Where did the children live?
3. What did Mother make for them?
4. How did they get to the beach?
5. What was the weather like?
6. What did they do at the seaside?
7. What time did they come home?
8. What were the children called?

 Number

Theme   To help with learning of tables – in this case the seven times table.

Materials   Mastercopy 15

 General Studies

Theme   To explain the rotation of the earth

Materials   Globe and netball (to represent the sun); Atlases

Method
1. Begin by discussing the rotation of the earth which gives us day and night. Then show how the earth moves on its axis so that some countries are nearer the sun (i.e. their summer) and other countries are further away (i.e. their winter).
2. Use an atlas to research weather patterns e.g. inches of rainfall and hours of sunshine in different countries.

 Art and Craft

Theme 1   Holidays

Method   Design a 'Come to Britain' poster. It should depict tourist attractions that are both natural and man-made.

Theme 2   The seaside

Materials   The poem 'Waves' below

Method   Make a picture in chalk, paint or crayon, or a material or paper collage to illustrate this poem.

> There are big waves and little waves, green waves and blue.
> Waves you can jump over, waves you jump through.
> Waves that rise up like a great water wall,
> Waves that swell softly and don't break at all.
> Waves that can whisper, waves that can roar,
> Tiny waves that run at you running on the shore.

Eleanor Farjeon

Physical Education

Theme   Bench ball

Method   Divide the class into two teams. Place a bench at either end of the hall with one child from each team acting as first catcher on the bench. Starting from the middle of the hall, the ball must be passed from player to player until it is caught by the catcher on the bench. The last player to throw the ball joins the catcher on the bench. The first team to have all its players standing on the bench is the winner.

 Movement and Drama

Theme 1   To dramatise music

Materials   The music 'Summertime' from *Porgy and Bess* by Gershwin

Method   Divide the children into groups of four and dramatise the gathering of cotton:
a. scything b. gathering c. passing d. stacking.

Theme 2   Drama situations
1. A family in a car stuck in traffic
2. A customs officer
3. Rescue at sea

UPPER JUNIORS

 Written Work and Language

Theme 1   To produce a proposal for class discussion:
'Is eight week's summer holiday too long?'

Method   Help the children to see both sides of the argument so that they can write their own speech for and against the motion – the best to be used in a class debate.

Theme 2   Descriptive writing – fact and fiction

Materials   Pictures cut from holiday brochures

Method   The children are each given a picture of a resort or hotel at home or abroad.
a. Their first task is to describe it as in a holiday brochure, ensuring that visitors would want to stay there.
b. They must write a factual description of the place – the sort of things the tourist would really like to know but is not always told.

 Number

Theme   Practice in the four rules

Materials   Squared paper. Mastercopies 16 and 6 (100 square)

Method   Draw a large square of 10 by 10 smaller squares or use Mastercopy 6. Shade in the answers to the sums on the sheet (Mastercopy 16) in the appropriate squares. This set of answers will make a sandcastle picture. If the children enjoy this activity they can be asked to make their own designs and the sums for them.

 General Studies

Theme   To show the relevance of sunlight in plant growth

Materials   Mastercopy 17

Important words
    Photosynthesis
    Carbon dioxide
    Oxygen
    Chlorophyll
    Carbohydrates (sugars and starch)

Method   Plants need to absorb carbon dioxide, water and salts in order to produce carbohydrates for growth. Land plants absorb carbon dioxide from the air and water from the soil. Sunlight provides the energy for the chemical process of change (photosynthesis) of these elements into carbohydrates. Sunlight is absorbed by the green pigment (chlorophyll) in the green parts (mainly leaves) of plants. As the plant needs only carbon dioxide, oxygen is given off as a by-product.
1. If there is time try growing seeds without light and note the results.
2. There are some simple experiments suitable for classroom use to test

for starch and to show that chlorophyll and sunlight are necessary for photosynthesis.

3. Remind children of what we need to breathe to live and what we exhale. Is it silly to talk to your plants?

 Art and Craft

Theme   To illustrate letters or words

Method   Use either the letters of the word 'summer' or the whole word to illustrate aspects of the season.

 Physical Education

Theme 1   Indoor rounders using an air ball

Theme 2   Snake tag

Method   Divide the class in half. Depending on the size of the area available work either with one group or both groups at the same time. The children hold each other round the waist. The aim is for the end of the 'snake' to tag the 'head' who is then out. This carries on until about five children are left.

 Movement and Drama

Theme   To link representative movements

Method   Divide the class into four groups. Each group is then given a set of five words to illustrate dramatically and link together.
1. sun, shimmer, sea, soak, sand.
2. warmth, waves, wearily, wandering, wide.
3. heat, hop, happy, hurried, heavy.
4. light, lift, laze, languid, lively.

QUICKIES

1. Ring the ten seaside towns.

T	E	N	B	Y	P	B	C	C
R	A	Y	R	D	E	A	L	S
U	L	J	I	G	N	X	A	L
R	Y	E	G	K	Z	M	C	R
O	R	D	H	U	A	A	T	H
D	A	O	T	W	N	I	O	Y
H	E	V	O	Q	C	S	N	L
Z	R	E	N	F	E	W	O	P
M	O	R	E	C	A	M	B	E

2. How many words can you find in three minutes from the word SANDCASTLE? There should be at least 30.

10 AUTUMN

INFANTS

 Written Work and Language

Theme   Learn a poem

Materials   Acorns, matchsticks (for pins), felt-tip pens; the poem 'Acorn Bill' below.

Method
1. Display the poem on the blackboard or on a large wall sheet. Ask the children to read it through and then learn it together.
2. You can make Acorn Bill as described in the text of the poem.

> *Acorn Bill*
> I made a little acorn man
> And inked his smiling face,
> I stuck four pins for legs and arms,
> Each firmly in its place.
>
> I found a tiny acorn cup
> To put upon his head,
> And then I showed him to my friends;
> 'Meet Acorn Bill,' I said.
>
> *Ruth Ainsworth*

 Number

Theme   Matching

Materials   Mastercopy 18

Method
1. Matching one to one. Identify the leaves on the top half of the sheet before the children do the exercise.
2. 'Apples under the tree'. The lower half of the sheet is for practice in matching correct numbers to apples.

 General Studies

Theme   To study leaves

Materials   Leaves; a story such as 'Why the Evergreen Trees keep their Leaves in Winter' from *How to tell stories to children* by E. Bryant.

Method   Explain the difference between deciduous and evergreen trees. Write the words in large letters on a piece of paper. Choose a random selection of leaves. Look at each one and notice its colour, texture and shape. Decide whether it comes from a deciduous tree or an evergreen. When the leaves are sorted, ask the children if the leaves in each pile have anything else in common.

 Art and Craft

Theme   Leaves

Materials   Green leaves, paint, tissue paper

Method
1. Printing with the leaves – always use the underside of the leaf as it is more heavily veined.
2. Collage of overlapping tissue paper leaves in autumnal colours – a leaf-shaped template would be useful here.

Physical Education

Theme   To practise landing

Method
1. Stress the importance of bending leg joints so as not to jar your body. On the spot, bend knees with heels on the floor. Then bend knees, bend ankles, bend toes.
2. Jump on the spot. Run and jump. Try running and leaping – how does the landing differ?
3. Get the children to practise bunny jumps as an alternative way to feel the 'bounce'.
4. If apparatus is available, use it in a way that lets the children experience and reinforce landing skills.

Movement and Drama

Theme   Spinning and falling

Method
1. Help the children to move using movement sentences.
   a. Spirals — slow, stationary — 'I reach up as high as I can and then slowly I turn round and round down to the ground.'
   b. Spirals — slow, moving — 'I am stretched up high and I can sink and slide and turn and spread.'
   c. Spirals — fast, stationary — 'I turn very fast on the spot keeping thin and tight.'
   d. Spirals — fast, moving — 'I whizz across the floor spinning round and round.'
2. After experimenting with these themes, talk about leaves in autumn and how they reach the ground. Perhaps the children could make an autumn movement sequence.

LOWER JUNIORS

 Written Work and Language

Theme   Comprehension

Materials   Mastercopy 19

Method
1. Read the information about the potato and then answer the questions.
2. This can be extended by making a list of all the vegetables the children can think of and categorising them into root or stem vegetables.

 Number

Theme   Work with the calendar

Method
1. Select the month in which you are doing this work and ask the following questions:-

a. I have to change a dental appointment from the 27th and make it twelve days earlier. What will be day and date?
b. If I go away on holiday on the 12th and return after ten days, what will the day and date be on my return?
c. If I go roller-skating on the first and third Saturday of the month, what will those dates be?
d. What will be the day and the date a fortnight from today?
e. How many weekends are there in this month? Give the dates.

2. Write these dates in numbers e.g. Sept. 16th–16/9
   a. October 31st   b. November 5th   c. December 25th
   d. November 25th   e. September 26th   f. September 4th
   g. September 29th   h. October 9th   i. December 2nd
   Some of these are very famous dates. Can you identify them?

3. Ask the children to write their own birth date in numbers giving date, month and year.

 General Studies

Theme   Autumn

Materials   A story such as 'The Blackberry Bush' from *Stories and Poems* by Celia Thaxter

Method   Although Autumn seems a sad time when the leaves fall and plants die down, it is a necessary part of the natural cycle of growth and regrowth. Explain this cycle simply to the children. Use the story to illustrate. Ask the children to illustrate a year's cycle of growth from what they can work out for themselves by thinking about trees (apple, horse-chestnut) and flowers (daffodils, crocuses) that they know.

 Art and Craft

Theme   Signs and Shades of Autumn

Method
1. Find one sign of Autumn. Create a picture around it – a seed, a leaf, a fruit, a bare twig.
2. Take a leaf-rubbing using kitchen paper and a thick wax crayon. Repeat the rubbings all over the page either at random or to create a leaf pattern. Remove the leaves and wash over the paper with a thin yellow colour wash.

3. Cover the paper with random crayonning in autumnal shades. Cover this with a complete layer of black crayonning. Using the end of a pen (preferably a used one) scratch through the black to reveal a picture underneath.

 Physical Education

Theme   Leaf tag

Method   Organise the children into two teams, one at either end of the room. Number them. Each person has a beanbag which is representative of a leaf. The children have to try to cross from one end of the room to the other when their number is called, balancing a beanbag on their head. They must reach the other side without being tagged by their opposite number and with the beanbag remaining on their head. If it falls off or they are tagged, they must return to their own team base. At the end, count to see how many of each team have successfully crossed the room with their 'leaf'.

 Movement and Drama

Theme   Body shape

Method   Get the children to recognise elementary body shapes. As the body extends into space it is large, as it comes into itself it is small. It can also be pin-like and piercing, flat and wall-like but still large. Small body shapes need curved spines, but the body need not only be ball-shaped, it can be twisted and curved. See if the children can use their experiences to translate leaf shape into body shape. e.g. spiky evergreens, curved oak leaves, pointed, prickly holly leaves.

UPPER JUNIORS

 Written Work and Language

Theme   Writing poetry from selected words

Materials   Autumn poetry: 'Ode to Autumn' by John Keats from the *Golden Treasury* and 'October' on the right.

Method   Read the poems to the children and ask them to select the autumnal words. Make a list of these and suggest that they recycle them into their own poems.

October

The Summer is over
The trees are all bare
There is mist in the garden
And frost in the air.
The meadows are empty
And gathered the sheaves –
But isn't it lovely
Kicking up leaves!

John from the garden
Has taken the chairs
It's dark in the evening
And cold on the stairs.
Winter is coming
And everyone grieves –
But isn't it lovely
Kicking up leaves.

Rose Fyleman

 Number

Theme   Time

Materials   Mastercopy 20

Method
1. Tell the children about Greenwich Mean Time. GMT is the basis of standard time throughout the world. The line of 0° longitude passes exactly through Greenwich, England. Standard time for different localities is worked out from this for particular meridians of longitude. Therefore the world is divided into time-zones either east or west of Greenwich.
2. If it were 12 noon at Greenwich, what time would it be in
   a. New York – 5 hours earlier
   b. Tokyo – 9 hours later
   c. Sydney – 10 hours later

d. Egypt – 2 hours later
e. Argentina – 3 hours earlier?

3. Use the world map, Mastercopy 20 to plot these places and see if you can find which line of longitude they are on.

 General Studies

Theme   Leaf fall

Materials   Horse-chestnut twigs give the clearest example
Important words – Deciduous, evergreen, terminal bud, lateral bud, axil, leaf scar, girdle scar.

Method   In Autumn the leaves of *deciduous* trees change colour. This is a sign that the cells of the leaf are breaking down chemically, the cell contents are digested and the soluble products are absorbed back into the tree. The leaf will dry up and fall off leaving a scar with a characteristic pattern of dots for each species of tree. The scar is made from corky tissue and protects the stem from the entry of bacteria. Above each *leaf scar* there should be a *lateral bud* ready for new growth the following spring. *Girdle scars* are the scars which extend part way round the twig. They show where the *terminal bud* scales fell off during growth in spring. Since they mark the position of each year's terminal bud they also show the amount of growth during the year.
       After explaining this to the children, make sure they understand the important words. Ask them to recount orally or in written form. If you can find some horse-chestnut twigs get the children to draw what they can see.

 Art and Craft

Theme   Leaf shapes

Method   Use a flat leaf as a template. With a thick dry brush and fairly thick paint, brush outward from the centre of the leaf, each brush stroke continuing over the edge of the leaf and gently onto the paper beneath. When the leaf is lifted off the paper there should be a clear space where it lay and a lightly defined pattern of its shape. Continue by repeating this technique all over the paper in a random pattern.

 Physical Education

Theme 1   'How fit are you?'

Method   Start with a good warm-up session of bending and stretching. Then, using one minute as the measured time span: how many sit-ups, stride jumps, squat thrusts and step-ups can the children do?

Theme 2   Tail-tag

Method   Divide children into twos. One partner has a band tucked into the back of their shorts. The partner has to retrieve the band. This can involve weaving and dodging exercises.

 Movement and Drama

Theme   A firework display

Method
1. Discuss with the children the different sorts of fireworks and how they could be portrayed in movement.
    a. Rockets – shooting upwards
    b. Catherine Wheels – circular movement of varying speed
    c. Waterfall – up into the air, then falling and spreading
    d. Shooting stars – short bursts of movement
    e. Parachutes – fast into the air and then falling gently
2. Practise the movements as a class before dividing into groups. Each group can represent a particular firework. Make a display using the group as a whole or individual members of the group.

(*Continued on page 50.*)

QUICKIES

1. The Americans call the Autumn the Fall. Test your reflexes with
    this paper that falls!
    Cut a piece of stiff paper or card 12 in × 2 in (30 cm × 5 cm)
    and mark it as shown. Hold the card at the top with one hand,
    let it drop and catch it with the other hand. Make a note of the
    number where you catch it. Have about six goes each. The one
    with the highest total is the winner.

0
1
2
3
4
5
6
7
8
9
10

2. Complete the following proverbs:-
    a. Make hay while the sun ....
    b. Too many cooks ....
    c. Out of sight, out of ....
    d. A bird in the hand ....
    e. A stitch in time ....
    f. People in glasshouses shouldn't ....
    Can you explain them?

3. Where do the following currencies come from?

Franc	Mark
Peseta	Guilder
Punt	Drachma
Lira	Kroner

11 WINTER

INFANTS

 Written Work and Language

Theme   Compound words

Materials   Mastercopy 21

Method   Use the Mastercopy for filling in the compound words. Then the pictures can be coloured. How many more compound words can the children remember?

 Number

Theme   Addition to ten

Materials   Mastercopy 21

Method   Use the Mastercopy. The children can colour the pictures to complete the page.

 General Studies

Theme   How cold temperatures change water vapour

Method
1. Winter is the coldest time of the year. We can see our breath as it leaves our bodies when we are outside. Water vapour in the breath changes into drops of water in the cold air – we say that it condenses. A good way of watching condensation occur is to cut a hole in a piece of cardboard. Hold the cardboard against a cold window and breathe through the hole. Watch what happens.
2. Go on to explain how snowflakes and ice crystals are formed. Snowflakes are formed from ice crystals which in turn are caused by water vapour in rising air cooling to below freezing point.

 Art and Craft

Theme 1   Snowflakes

Method   Use a sponge dipped in thick white paint to print snowflakes onto coloured or black paper.

Theme 2   Make a snowman

Materials   Cardboard tubes for the body, cotton wool for the head, buttons for the coat and coloured paper to make features and a hat.

Method   Paint the tube first, then cut coloured paper shapes while it is drying.

Theme 3   Snowmen mobiles

Materials   2 paper circles, 1 hat-shaped template, scraps of coloured paper, thread and glue.

Method   See illustration

Physical Education

Theme Keeping warm

Method
1. Explain that the three basic methods of getting warm are rubbing, shaking and slapping. Get the children to lie down, relax and be still for a few minutes; (it's normally cold in the hall anyway!). See how many can easily touch their toes, skip and stretch to the ceiling. Run through these exercises to see if they make a difference.
   a. Rub hands together, repeat with feet
   b. Shake out hand, then arm, repeat on the other side
   c. Sit with legs out in front, gently slap legs up and down
   d. In pairs rub each other's backs
   e. Stand, shake body down to floor and back up again
   Use variations on these exercises and then check touching toes, skipping and stretching.
2. Change the words of 'Ten Green Bottles' to 'Ten White Snowmen Shivering in the Snow'.

 Movement and Drama

Theme Contrasts of movement

Materials Verse from 'On a Night of Snow' from the '*Book of Young Verse*' (Armada Lion) – see below.

Method Let the children work as individuals. Only bring in the poem at the end. Begin with stretching, arching, curling and uncurling, leaping and spinning. Intersperse all the actions with stillness and remember to encourage different directions and levels.

'On a Night of Snow'

Cat, if you go outdoors you must walk in the snow,
You will come back with little white shoes on your feet,
Like white slippers of snow that have heels of sleet.
Stay by the fire, my Cat. Lie still, do not go.
See how the flames are leaping and hissing low.
I will bring you a saucer of milk like a marguerite,
So white and so smooth, so spherical and so sweet.
Stay with me, Cat. Outdoors the wild winds blow.

Elizabeth Coatsworth

LOWER JUNIORS

 Written Work and Language

Theme Expressive writing

Method Choose a winter word that isn't too long e.g. 'snow'. The children write the letters of the word one under the other down the page and then put a line of writing after each letter. It can be poetic, descriptive of the word or narrative but each line must begin with its corresponding letter. The children can decorate the first letter of each line to pick out the word, cut round the shape and mount the work on black or coloured paper.

 Number

Theme Temperature

Materials Classroom thermometer(s)

Method
1. Use the diagram below to draw a larger version of the thermometer on a piece of paper. Mark Celsius (Centigrade) readings on one side and Fahrenheit on the other. The children can use this to make their own diagram.
2. Using a thermometer take the following temperatures and write them down:-
   a. Inside the classroom
   b. Outdoors
   c. In the school hall
   d. In the school kitchen (if possible)
3. Ask the children to find out about the following temperatures and mark them in on their diagram:-
   1. Body temperature
   2. The freezing point of water
   3. The boiling point of water
   4. The minimum legal requirement for a working environment

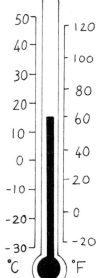

General Studies

Theme   Snow

Method   Three conditions are necessary for snow to form:-
1. When the air can no longer hold any more water vapour
2. When the temperature is below 10 °F
3. If there are tiny solid particles in the upper air around which the snow can form
    When these three conditions occur the molecules of water form around the particle and stick together to form an ice crystal. As the crystal floats down, more water molecules stick to it making it larger. Several of these crystals stick together to make a snowflake. Get the children to find out more about snow and let them practise drawing a six-pointed snowflake (see Mastercopy 21).

 Art and Craft

Theme   Snow

Method
1. White chalk drawing on black paper makes an effective winter picture.
2. Use the diagram and instructions to fold and cut an accurate snowflake.

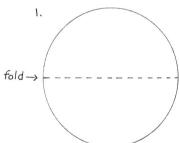
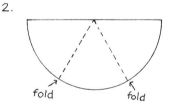
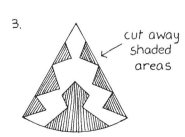
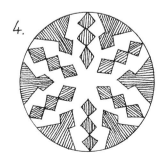

cut away shaded areas

 Physical Education

Theme   Hoppity

Method   All but one child stand in a circle facing inwards. The extra child stands in the middle. On a signal he hops outside the ring and hops round in a clockwise direction. He chooses someone and taps them on the shoulder. This child hops round the circle in the opposite direction and the first one to get to the empty space is safe. The other goes to the centre of the circle to begin again. The game can be varied by using different methods of movement.

 Movement and Drama

Theme   Exploring a given situation

Method
1. Tell the children that there is a box in front of them. Can they find out about the box – how big it is, what shape it is, is it heavy? Make the first exploration a silent one.
2. Change the experience. Let the children pretend to be inside the box. How do they feel – is it closed, are they alone, can they make a sound on the walls?

UPPER JUNIORS

 Written Work and Language

Theme   Verb tenses – past, present and future

Materials   *A Christmas Carol* by Charles Dickens

Method
1. Repeat the story. This will get the children thinking along the lines of past, present and future.
2. Give the children three completed sentences, one in each tense. They must add the other two tenses for each sentence. Here are three starter sentences:-
    a. Last winter I went sledging.
    b. It is cold today, I am shivering.
    c. In the future I will behave myself.

Number

Theme Problem solving: temperature/time

Method Mother and father have frozen most of the Christmas dinner but want it all to arrive on the table at the right time. Help them to work out a timetable of when to start thawing out the food and when to start cooking it and see if you can arrange for Christmas dinner to be served at 1 pm on Christmas Day.

Turkey 12 lb frozen, needs 36 hours to thaw in refrigerator. Cook (stuffed weight 14 lb) for 40 mins at 220 °C, $3\frac{1}{2}$ hours at 170 °C and 30 mins at 200 °C to make the skin crisp.

Sausages Cook from frozen but need 1 hour dividing heat between low and high

Potatoes Roast for $1\frac{1}{2}$ hours, the last part at a high heat

Sprouts Cook from frozen in boiling water for 8 mins

Peas Cook from frozen in boiling water for 5 mins

Cranberry sauce Frozen, thaw at room temperature for 3 hours

Iced Christmas pudding Thaw for 15 mins. Decorate with cream

Traditional Pudding Needs to steam for 2 hours

Brandy butter Thaw for 3 hours

 General Studies

Theme Snow line

Materials Mastercopy 20 (World map)

Method

1. Explain that though snow is formed in the upper atmosphere very little reaches the earth as snow, but it does reach the earth as rain due to the rise in temperature nearer earth. At sea level, in the equatorial belt, it never snows because of the warmer temperatures, though snow will fall on high mountains or heavy rainfall turn to snow. The higher the altitude the colder the temperature therefore the highest regions of the earth can have snow all the year round (Alps, Himalayas). You can draw a line across high mountains which divides snow-covered areas from bare ground. This snow line will move in winter and summer.

2. Ask the children to mark in on the Mastercopy the highest mountains of the world that have snow lines. Mark in the equatorial belt where it never snows at sea level.

 Art and Craft

Theme 1 Silver foil pictures

Materials Card, string, foil and glue, shoe polish

Method Make a picture or wintry pattern by sticking the string onto the card with glue. Cover the picture with scrunched-up foil – this avoids tearing the foil. Secure the foil at the back. Press down around the string with fingers to raise the pattern. To get a pewter effect, brush all over the picture with black shoe polish and then use another brush to polish it off. These pictures can be made with gold foil and brown polish and are also very effective using leaves or seeds instead of string.

Theme 2 Hand patterns

Method Get the children to spread out their hands on either white paper or newspaper. Draw round the hands and cut them out. These can then be mounted on black paper and arranged in patterns.

 Physical Education

Theme 1 Wounded soldier

Method The teacher stands in the middle of a circle and throws the ball to each child in turn. If children miss the ball they must pay a penalty (go down on one knee). Next time round if they miss they pay a further penalty (go down on two knees) but if they catch the ball they can stand up again.

Theme 2 Hand ball

Materials Each team will need a ball or beanbag.

Method Mark two parallel lines 3 m apart. Divide the class into equal teams and line them up with the leaders facing their teams on one line and the second players at the head of the teams on the other. (See page 55.)

```
4 ○      ×      △      □
3 ○      ×      △      □
2 ○      ×      △      □
_____

              ↑
             3m
              ↓
_____

1 ○      ×      △      □
```

On a signal the leaders pass the ball to the second players who run round the team and back to their places, throw the ball back to their leaders and crouch down so as not to interfere with play. The leaders throw the ball to each of their players in turn and the last players, after completing their runs, pass it back to their leaders. The game may be lengthened by pat-bouncing the ball during the run. Each player may also in turn occupy the place of the leader. The game is then finished when the leaders have worked their way back to their original starting points.

 Movement and Drama

Theme   Poetry

Materials   The poem 'Winter' below

Method   Use the poem as a starting point. Read it to the class and discuss the wintry feel of the words and images it presents. Divide the class so that the children can learn parts and dramatise parts to make a whole.

Winter

> When icicles hang by the wall
> And Dick the shepherd blows his nail,
> And Tom bears logs into the hall,
> And milk comes frozen home in pail;
> When blood is nipt, and ways be foul,
> Then nightly sings the staring owl
> Tuwhoo!
> Tuwhit! Tuwhoo! A merry note!
> While greasy Joan doth keel the pot.

> When all around the wind doth blow,
> And coughing drowns the parson's saw,
> And birds sit brooding in the snow,
> And Marian's nose looks red and raw;
> When roasted crabs hiss in the bowl —
> Then nightly sings the staring owl
> Tuwhoo!
> Tuwhit! Tuwhoo! A merry note!
> While greasy Joan doth keel the pot.
>
> *William Shakespeare*

QUICKIES

A Winter Quiz

1. Where are the next Winter Olympics to be held?
2. What is the name of the race of people who live in igloos?
3. A tortoise _____ during the winter months.
4. Bing Crosby sang a very famous song called 'White _____'
5. Make six words beginning with 'w' from the word 'winter'. (win, wet, wit, went, writ, weir)
6. Swallows _____ in winter.
7. When it is winter in England, what season is it in Australia?
8. How many words that rhyme with 'winter' can you write down?
9. Is the North Pole in the Arctic or the Antarctic?
10. How many points has a snowflake?

12 WATER

INFANTS

 Written Work and Language

Theme   To explore and illustrate one day's use of water

Materials   One sheet of A4 paper per child (folded into quarters)

Method   Class discussion to elicit ideas from the children as to how the family uses water during each day e.g. washing, cooking, watering plants, painting, water play, swimming. Ask the children to draw four uses of water on their paper. A simple explanatory sentence may be added to each picture.

 Number

Theme   To show the difference between things that sink and things that float

Materials   Clear bowl/tank of water; scissors, paper for drawing and for mounting

Method   After a demonstration using available materials that sink or float, discuss with the children any alternative objects or fluids they might suggest. The children then choose one of each type to draw and cut out. Assemble this as a class picture.

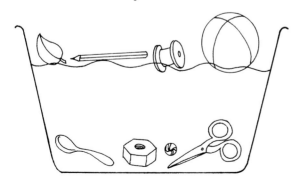

 General Studies

Theme   Basic weather cycle

Materials   Mastercopy 22

Method   Explain the weather cycle to the children and relate it to their copy of the diagram. Children colour and add detail. An extension to this could be a simple daily weather chart.

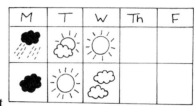

 Art and Craft

Theme   Watery pictures

Method
1. Spatter pictures with limited colours
2. Blot and fold 'butterfly' pictures (see page 27)
3. Rainy day pictures
4. 'What I need to wear when it rains.'

 Physical Education

Theme   Shipwreck

Materials   Hoops

Method   Scattered hoops are islands of safety when the signal to stop is given. Vary movements between hoops, e.g. hop, walk, run.

Movement and Drama

Theme   Pathways using stream → river → sea

Method   A stream rushes straight along. A river slows down and winds on its way to the sea. The sea is collective, rhythmic and changeable. Combine these movements for a class movement sequence.

LOWER JUNIORS

 Written Work and Language

Theme   Imaginative use of descriptive words

Materials   Poems 'The washing machine' and 'Happiness' below

Method   Introduce the poems to the class noting the difference between made-up and ordinary descriptive words and style of presentation. Using water as a theme, get the children to experiment by making lists of words which can later be incorporated into their own poems.

The washing machine

It goes fwunkety
　　then shlunkety,
as the washing goes around.

The water spluncheses
　　and it schluncheses,
as the washing goes around.

As you pick it out it splocheses,
　　then it flocheses,
as the washing goes around.

But at the end it schlopperies,
　　and then flopperies,
and the washing stops going round.

Jeffrey Davies

Happiness

John had Great Big Waterproof Boots on;
John had a Great Big Waterproof Hat;
John had a Great Big Waterproof Mackintosh —
And that (Said John) Is That.

A.A. Milne

 Number

Theme   Problem-solving using basic operations + and ×.

Method   Present the problem.
'If, in the tropical rain forests, the daily rainfall is 3 cm in the months of October–March and 5 cm for the rest of the year, calculate
1. Each month's rainfall
2. Which six-month period has the highest rainfall
3. Yearly rainfall
4. Which three months have the highest rainfall
5. Which two months have the lowest rainfall

 General Studies

Theme   To show the passage of water from reservoir to tap

Materials   Mastercopy 23

Method   Recap on the basic weather cycle (see Infant section on page 56). Discuss how water gets into taps. Encourage the children's knowledge of local reservoirs and sewerage plants.

 Art and Craft

Theme 1   Raindrop collage

Method   Using templates for drops in varying sizes, cut out shapes from magazines or coloured paper and arrange them to make individual pictures.

Theme 2   Illustrate 'The Story of Semmerwater' on page 58

Theme 3   Bubble pictures

Materials   Washing-up liquid in yoghurt or margarine pots with powder paint and a little water

Method   Blow through a straw and place paper gently over the top to take a print. (See also on page 73.)

Physical Education

Theme   Team Dodgeball

Method   Two teams line up an arm's length apart. Each team leader holds a netball. On a signal they dodge between their team to the end, run down the centre, return to their place and pass the ball to the next in line. They then weave in and out of their team and so on until the ball comes back to the team leaders.

 Movement and Drama

Theme   Mime with water links

Method   Take turns to mime an activity associated with water e.g. brushing teeth, washing hands.

The Story of Semmerwater

It is about a town in Yorkshire. At first the town is small, the townsfolk simple people, with time to listen to the voice of the river that flows under the bridges of their streets, time to sit on the river bank in the evenings and talk to each other, time to worship in the church on Sundays. As the years go by the townsfolk prosper and enlarge the town. The baron builds a castle, the priest a richly decorated church, the people, noble houses. They dress and eat well. They work hard to earn more money, they enjoy themselves. Their time is absorbed in making and enjoying wealth. The splendid church is empty and dark, neglected even by the priest. The townspeople no longer have time to go to church, no longer have time to listen to the voice of the river, no longer have time to look up at the hills encircling the town. One day a beggar arrives. He asks a shoemaker to mend his sandals, a baker to give him bread, the baron's cook to draw him water from the castle well, and the priest for a place to sleep. No one will help him; they are too busy, too mean, too proud, too indifferent. Sadly, the beggar goes away. As he climbs the hillside he meets a shepherd. The shepherd is poor, he has a wife and seven children to keep, but the family courteously share their supper and the shelter of their hut with the old man. In the morning they receive their simple reward, and the beggar is revealed as an angel, who causes the sky to darken with

---

storms, the streams to swell in angry torrents, the river to rise and form a lake which drowns the city.

In summer nowadays there is water-skiing on the lake, but when it lies cold and quiet under the bare hills in winter sunshine it has a bleak and lonely aspect.

UPPER JUNIORS

 Written Work and Language

Theme   Word-building skills and dictionary work

pre⬚cipit⬚ation   f⬚lui⬚d

ra⬚inf⬚all   a⬚quari⬚um

si⬚nk⬚   res⬚erv⬚oir

f⬚loa⬚t   d⬚yk⬚e

Method   Give children the letters in the squares and explain that they are part of a word and cannot be rearranged or changed. The words are generally linked to water. Get the children to find the correct words. Oral clues may be given e.g. total number of letters in the word. Write one sentence for each word to illustrate its meaning.

 Number

Theme   To revise area

Materials   Mastercopy 24; cm² paper.

Method   Using the illustration get the children to work out:-
1. The area of the island by counting the squares
2. The area of the lagoon
3. The area of the lake
   They can then create an island of their own with a given area and lake, river and forest.

 General Studies

Theme   To create a flow diagram related to water

Method   Explain the use of flow diagrams, logic sequencing and relate this to computer programming. Try this simple diagram with them.

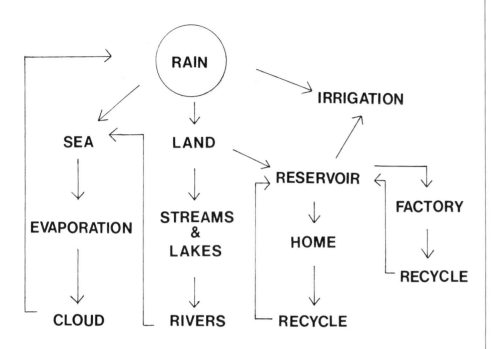

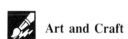   **Art and Craft**

Theme   Use the story of Noah's Ark as an inspiration. (Genesis 6–10. Also *Macdonald Bible Stories No. 3. Noah and the Ark* and *Noah's Ark* – Random House) The children can choose to draw:-
1. The exterior of the Ark
2. The interior of the Ark
3. The flood
4. The return of the dove
5. Mount Ararat
6. Unloading the Ark
7. The rainbow

   Physical Education

Theme   Team Dodgeball as for Lower Juniors on page 58 but increase the difficulty

Method
1. Each child moves backward instead of forward to weave and dodge between the team.
2. They bounce the ball while moving instead of holding it.

   Movement and Drama

Theme   Situation improvisation in small groups

Method   Give the groups these situations:
1. 'Shipwrecked'   a.   Be stranded survivors on an island.
     b.   Be survivors in a lifeboat.
2. 'In the Ark'   Encourage humour – children must be animals as well as people.
3. 'Flood'   Can they improvise a domestic drama such as a burst pipe or overflowing basin?

QUICKIES

1. Where are the Ocean of Storms and the Sea of Rains?
2. Who went to sea in a sieve?
3. What sort of water is an iceberg made of?
4. Name six water sports.
5. Which is the longest river in the world? (Nile)
6. Complete the rhyme: 'Doctor Foster went to Gloucester' . . . .
7. Name three lakes.
8. What is the ship called that moves under water?
9. Who crossed the Atlantic Ocean in the 'Mayflower'?
10. What kind of ship has a runway for aircraft on it?

13 FOOD

INFANTS

 Written Work and Language

Theme   Alphabet work and phonics

Method   As a class, go through the alphabet; stress the sound of each letter. Can the children find a food for each letter of the alphabet? This can be illustrated either in a frieze or by individual work.

 Number

Theme   Number food

Materials   Mastercopy 25

Method
1. Use as many number rhymes as you can think of that mention food e.g.
   5 currant buns
   5 fat sausages
   5 little peas
   1 potato, 2 potato
2. Each child can first cut out and decorate a cardboard mat. Use the Mastercopy to cut out a plate, knife, fork and spoons. The children then have to lay the table correctly on their mat. They can draw a meal on the plate but try to make sure they know whether it is breakfast, dinner or tea.
3. Using the Mastercopy, the teacher gives oral instructions and the children must link the child with his or her shopping e.g. Shaun bought some apples.

 General Studies

Theme   'What food is good for you?'

Materials   A simple book on food can be helpful – most schools have one in the library; magazines.

Method   Talk to the children about food and why we need certain kinds in a balanced diet. We need:
1. food for growth – meat, cheese, fish, eggs
2. food for energy – sugar, starch, butter
3. food for health – green vegetables, fruit, nuts, whole fibres, pulses
   Make a chart with these three headings and see if the children can find pictures of food to put in the right columns.

 Art and Craft

Theme   *The Very Hungry Caterpillar* by Eric Carle (Puffin)

Materials   Sugar paper, tissue paper, pictures of fruit

Method   Make a frieze of the story of the hungry caterpillar. Make the caterpillar from circles of sugar paper or overlapping tissue paper. Add the head, tail, feet. The caterpillar ate 1 apple, 2 pears, 3 plums, 4 strawberries, 5 oranges and whatever the children choose to draw for Saturday. He had a large leaf on Sunday. Each food should have a hole in it where the caterpillar has been eating it.

 Physical Education

Theme   Working with balls

Method
1. Start the lesson with the children in pairs, throwing and catching with a large ball. If they are fairly proficient change to using smaller balls.
2. Place the children in a circle and give them each a number. The teacher calls out the number and that child must catch the ball thrown from the middle of the circle by the teacher. If they miss the ball, they sit down. The last one left standing is the winner.
3. Put the children into small groups to play 'Hot Potato'. The ball must be thrown within the group from child to child without being dropped. Let the children count how many times they can pass the Hot Potato.

 Movement and Drama

Theme   'Let's bake a cake'

Method   Give the basic ingredients of the cake separate movement themes which can be practised by the class individually. When you and they are satisfied, create a class 'cookery session'. Give narration to help with phrasing of movements and let the children choose appropriate words as sounds to accompany their movement.

e.g. eggs – gliding, sliding in $\frac{3}{4}$ rhythm

flour – floating, wavelike in $\frac{4}{4}$ rhythm

sultanas – short, stabbing, strong in $\frac{2}{4}$ rhythm

sugar – flowing, encompassing in $\frac{4}{4}$ rhythm

Simple plan

1. Four groups for ingredients
2. Six children form bowl/oven/tin
3. Two children are cooks
4. Bowl and cooks in centre
5. Ingredients move to them
6. Dense mixing, cooking, baking motifs (small→large group shape)

LOWER JUNIORS

 Written Work and Language

Theme   Imaginative writing

Method   Ask the children if they could choose three people, living or dead, to invite to dinner at their house, who would they choose? They must give the reasons for their choice and plan a menu which they think the guests would enjoy.

 Number

Theme   Using tabled information

Materials   Mastercopy 26

Method   Answer the questions using the information from the table on the Mastercopy. Add more questions as you like.

 General Studies

Theme   Components of food

Method   Food is made up of three basic properties – proteins, carbohydrates and fats.

1. Proteins are body-building.
2. Carbohydrates give body heat and energy.
3. Fats help the normal functioning of the body.
   Included in each of these are vitamins and minerals.
   a. Vitamins A, B, C, D and E help normal growth and healthy development.
   b. Minerals – iron, calcium, sodium and potassium need to be replenished.

Using pictures of food, ask the children to categorise it into the groups needed for a balanced diet. See if there are any books in the library to increase knowledge.

 Art and Craft

Theme 1   Potato prints. These are perhaps better left until you know the school fairly well as they require a fair amount of preparation and organisation.

Theme 2   Paint a pudding to eat at a party.

 Physical Education

Theme   Circle stride ball

Method   The children stand in a circle, feet apart and touching the person on either side. The ball is in the middle of the circle. The children use their hands to prevent the ball leaving the circle through their legs. If the ball goes out of the circle, a goal is scored and the child whose legs it passed has to leave the circle and become a catcher on the outside until the game starts again.

 Movement and Drama

Theme   Whole-body movements stressing effort and weight qualities

Method   Take the simple actions used in cooking and translate them into larger whole-body movements. Get the children to do each movement before experimenting with the whole-body movement.

1. Rolling pastry – fine touch, sustained→gathering movements, undulating, circular pathways
2. Whipping and beating – firm touch, sudden → spinning, asymmetric movement, speed

(*Continued on page 62*)

3. Kneading dough – firm touch, sustained → spinal movement, arching and twisting, tension, earthbound movements

UPPER JUNIORS

 Written Work and Language

Theme Menu-writing

Method Ask the children to imagine that they own a restaurant and serve certain dishes. The menu requires a detailed, mouth-watering description of the each dish. This can be done in a sentence but each noun used must have a pertinent adjective

e.g. 'Curry – separate chunks of tender meat in a fragrant sauce of exotic spices from the Indian continent, served with fluffy rice and crisp poppadums.'

Some dishes the children might like to describe are listed below – some can have a double meaning!

Shepherds Pie   Toad-in-the-Hole
Beef Wellington   Steak and Kidney Pudding
Sweet and Sour Pork   Fisherman's Pie
Baked Stuffed Potatoes   Knickerbocker Glory
Banana Split   Strawberry Mousse

 Number

Theme Price comparison

Materials Mastercopy 27

Method From the information on the sheet ask the children to find in each case the best value for price and size.

 General Studies

Theme Food breakdown in the body

Method Man eats for three main reasons:

1. To compensate for losses of living matter used up each day by natural processes
2. To provide material for growth
3. To obtain energy

The human body is made up of many elements but there are four main ones: – oxygen 66%, carbon 17%, hydrogen 10% and nitrogen 3%. Man cannot replace these elements directly but a balanced diet of carbohydrates, proteins and fats will provide all that is necessary. Carbohydrates and fats contain carbon, hydrogen and oxygen. Proteins have nitrogen and some other elements as well. All the elements mentioned can provide energy but only proteins can provide the basic requirements for the replacement of old tissue and the growth of new.

a. Ask the children to write down everything they ate on a previous day. See if this was a 'balanced' diet. Use information from Infant and Lower Junior General Studies on pages 60–61 to help in categorising the food.

b. Expand the theme by talking about the energy value of food as expressed in calories. How many calories does the body need at various stages of development and activity?

 Art and Craft

Theme Design inspired by food

Method

1. Design a menu for a very smart restaurant or a French Bistro.
2. If possible take an apple or a tomato into school. Cut it in half and let the children draw exactly the shapes that they see. This can be extended by translating the literal drawing into a design or pattern.

 Physical Education

Theme 1 Circle stride ball (see Lower Junior section on page 61)

Theme 2 Eggs and Bacon

Method All but two of the children stand in pairs, one behind the other, facing into a circle. One of the other two players is Bacon and he or she stands in the circle. The other, Eggs, goes outside the circle. On the signal Eggs runs either way round the circle, changing direction as often as he or she likes, while Bacon keeps close to him without leaving the circle. When Eggs sees his chance he comes into the circle and stands in front of a pair before being tagged by Bacon. When Eggs turns a pair into a group of three the player at the back become Eggs and the game begins again. If Bacon tags Eggs before he stands in front of a pair, Eggs becomes Bacon, while Bacon runs to any pair he chooses, stands in front and the player at the back becomes the new Eggs.

 Movement and Drama

Theme   Dramatic situations

Method   Mealtimes can provide instant drama. Get the children to improvise within the given situation. Some general discussion is needed beforehand.
1. The romantic dinner for two
2. Christmas lunch with large family of old and young
3. Husband coming home too late for evening meal
4. Mother feeding children something 'good for you'
5. Dinner party where food is a disaster
6. Tea with the Vicar

QUICKIES

1. How many songs can you think of (or sing) that include food in the title or opening verse? e.g.

   'Food, glorious food'
   'Boiled beef and carrots'

2. Try and make a crossword starting with the word 'eggs' and then adding the ways to cook them.

E	G	G	S		F
			C		R
			R		I
P	O	A	C	H	E	D
			M		D
			B
B	O	I	L	E	D
			E
			D

3. What items of food do you associate with:
   a. Devon   e. Melton Mowbray
   b. Cheddar   f. Bakewell
   c. Eccles   g. Edinburgh
   d. Bath   h. Dundee
4. What happened at the Boston Tea Party?

14 SIGNS, SYMBOLS AND SIGNALS

INFANTS

 Written Work and Language

Theme   Picture language

Materials   Large illustrations as below

Method   Using the illustrations, get the children to obey instructions without the need for speech. The children could then think up their own very simple picture instructions.

 Number

Theme   Using dice and dominoes to match with numbers

Materials   Large dice, set of dominoes

Method
1. Match a numeral card to the number of spots on throws of the dice.
2. For older infants – by throwing the dice twice and noting the number, make up plus or minus sums. With the dominoes use the two sets of spots on each to make up sums.

 General Studies

Theme   Animal, bird and human prints

Method   Show the children how animals, birds and humans are recognisable by their footprints. If possible go outside to see if they can find any evidence. All shoes make a different print. These can be illustrated by getting the children to walk on paper with their shoes on.

 Art and Craft

Theme   Street signs, symbols and signals

Method
1. Large painting of the school 'lollipop lady'
2. Picture of traffic lights showing their colours and sequences and where they stand
3. Painting of a Pelican crossing sign – choose whether it shows 'walk' or 'don't walk'

 Physical Education

Theme   Relay race

Materials   Large pictures of actions

Method   Organise the teams. Explain that each leg of the relay will be different and governed by the picture you hold up e.g. hop, jump, skip etc.

 Movement and Drama

Theme   Follow-my-Leader

Method   Use whole-body movements – stepping, hopping, jumping, leaping, turning, falling. Create a movement sequence for the children to follow and execute on their own.

LOWER JUNIORS

 Written Work and Language

Theme   Picture language

Method   Write a short story using pictures instead of words wherever possible.

 Number

Theme   Revision of words meaning + × − ÷ > < =

Materials   Mastercopy 28

Method   Ask the children to rewrite the sums using numbers and symbols before giving the answer.

 General Studies

Theme   Sending signals

Materials   Resource books about flags and signalling. Mastercopy 29

Method   Talk about the different ways that messages have been sent over the ages without the need for words.
1. Indian smoke signals
2. Mirrors
3. Morse code
4. Flag messages on ships
5. Semaphore signalling
6. Cub and Scout tracking signs
   A lot of this work may be extended by the children doing their own library research into different topics. They may be able to make up their own method of passing messages without words.

 Art and Craft

Theme 1   Family Shields

Materials   A book about heraldry, such as No. 19 in Ladybird Learnabouts Series 634.

Method   If possible use the book to give the children some idea of the design of family shields and mottoes. Then ask them to design a shield for their own family. Start with a basic shield shape, quarter it and fill each quarter with representative pictures relevant to the family's employment, name and leisure pursuits. Add a suitable motto underneath.

Theme 2   Design from signs

Method   Take any sign e.g. an arrow and make a design with it. This could then be used for printing either on paper or fabric if the necessary facilities are to hand.

 Physical Education

Theme   Actions race

Materials   Pack of action cards with appropriate words (hop, skip, jump, spin)

Method   Divide the class into two teams who stand facing each other with the pack of cards in the central space. One child from the opposite end of each team races to the middle and turns over a card; they have to complete a circle of their team and return to their own place doing the action on the card. The next child then runs to the middle and so on until all the team have had a turn.

 Movement and Drama

Theme   Free flow and bound flow

Method
1. Explain the difference between 'free flow' (continuous, uncontrolled, going) and 'bound flow' (restrained, careful, stopping). Get the children to experience the first by moving without stopping, travelling, rolling, spinning, then try the bound flow from static through short movements with stops and starts. Use a sign to control the stops. When the difference between the two has been mastered make movement sequences using both.

2. How does it feel? As an alternative or light relief, get the children in pairs. One is to move freely, the other may choose to stop or not to stop them. Does movement always become bound in the expectation of being stopped?

3. As a class activity with a pre-set signal to be given by the leader – an outward facing circle with two or three children running round the outside is a useful formation.

UPPER JUNIORS

 Written Work and Language

Theme   To revise punctuation signs.

Materials   Passage below

Method

1. Introduce the passage below as being from Alexander McKee's *How We found the Mary Rose* and explain that he was one of the original divers who wanted to find the *Mary Rose*. The difficulty had always been to find the exact location of the wreck. He had already spent many months on this work and was in competition with another group engaged on the same project. Although there was no co-operation between the groups, they agreed to compare nautical charts in an effort to pin-point the original siting of the wreck of the *Mary Rose*.

2. The passage for punctuation follows. Capital letters can also be left out when it is given to the children. We feel that they must be given some explanation of the dramatic necessity of starting a sentence with 'And' as this is not considered to be grammatically correct.

The charts were large and stiff and had to be held down at the corners by heavy weights. Sheringham's chart was unrolled and Towse and I leaned forward over the table, taking in the red cross and name Royal George (in 12 fathoms, not 14 after all), then sliding down to the right to where we saw the red cross and the name Edgar in 12–13 fathoms as we expected; and finally, almost automatically, going back to the Royal George and then looking up in the north-east arc towards the shallows of Spit Sand into our own search area. And there it was. A red inked cross and the name *Mary Rose*, in six fathoms. Towse gave an audible gasp.

Alexander McKee

 Number

Theme   Putting missing symbols into sums

Method   The children must work out the sum and find out which symbol has been left out. We have included one or two sums with brackets for the more able children. All four basic rule signs have been used.
This activity can be extended by letting the children work out their own sums without signs and giving them to a friend to complete.

1. 6 ☐ 5 = 11
2. 10 ☐ 3 = 7
3. 3 ☐ 4 = 12
4. 24 ☐ 6 = 4
5. 12 ☐ 6 = 18
6. 11 ☐ 4 = 7
7. 8 ☐ 6 = 48
8. 18 ☐ 9 = 2
9. 3 ☐ 6 = 10 ☐ 8
10. 12 ☐ 3 = 4 ☐ 5
11. 7 ☐ 7 = 50 ☐ 1
12. 7 ☐ 9 = 4 ☐ 4
13. 9 ☐ 6 = 34 ☐ 20
14. 6 ☐ 4 = 8 ☐ 3
15. (1 ☐ 7) ☐ 5 = 12
16. (9 ☐ 4) ☐ 6 = 30
17. (4 ☐ 3) ☐ 2 = 6
18. (7 ☐ 8) ☐ 6 = 62
19. (8 ☐ 9) ☐ 9 = 8
20. (6 ☐ 4) ☐ 2 = 5

 General Studies

Theme   Using maps

Materials   An ordnance survey map, preferably of the local area

Method   Use the map to find and make a list of the most common signs and symbols that can be seen. The children can then make a map of an area from an oral or written description. This would also entail the use of compass bearings.

 Art and Craft

Theme   Abstract painting

Method   Using no less than three colours, depict any of these concepts without using definable shapes.

Anger	Happiness
Despair	Love
Pain	Speed

 Physical Education

Theme   Beanbag tag

Materials Floor chalk; two colours of beanbags

Method Make two teams with equal amounts of beanbags. Draw three lines:- one central and one at either end of the hall with a small 'prison' space behind. Line the teams up, each with its own area and its own 'prison' area which contains its particular colour of beanbags. The object is to capture the other team's beanbags and take as many prisoners as possible.

Rules
1. Opposing sides can only tag in their own territory.
2. Tagged children are prisoners and remain behind prison line.
3. Prisoners can be freed by one of their own side.
4. Prisoners being freed must hold hands with their rescuer until they get back to their side. They cannot be tagged as long as they hold hands.
5. If any child captures a beanbag, it gives them free passage to their own area.

 Movement and Drama

Theme 'Anything You Can Do . . . .'

Method
1. Children, in pairs to start with, work on copying movements precisely. One child makes a short movement sequence for the other to copy. Reverse the situation. Get the children to work out sounds that catch the rhythm of the movement (staccato, legato).
2. Repeat the sequences with the added sounds. Emphasise the quality of the movements. Are they gentle, aggressive, cheeky, persuasive?
3. Maybe, having explored all these things, the children will want to make up a new sequence. Can the new sequence ask or demand something? Can the partners reply with their own sequence?

QUICKIES

1. Identify the following signs.

2. Sums by tapping. Tell the children first whether the sum is +, −, ÷ or ×. Tap out two separate numbers, children to work out answers.
3. *Winking Murder* (See also on page 18.)
   Children sit in a circle. A number of playing cards are dealt out including one Queen and one Jack. The child who gets the Queen is the detective. He declares himself while everyone is silent. The child with the Jack is the murderer, who kills his victims by winking at them. The detective has to name the murderer.
4. Composition of the Union flag; use Mastercopy 30.
5. Symbol sums; use Mastercopy 31. Each shape equals the same number each time. When you add them up they give the answers shown.

15 SHAPE

INFANTS

 Written Work and Language

Theme 1   Shape words

Materials   Pre-cut shapes (circle, square, triangle, rectangle) large enough for display

Method   Get the children to think about the shape of things around them and look in magazines and newspapers. Ask them to write down the objects or cut out the pictures of things that are a definite shape, sort out the words and pictures and glue them to the correct shape.

Theme 2   Digraph 'sh'

Method   Introduce the sound 'sh' and show how it is made up. Find or draw pictures of things that begin with 'sh'. Mount them in raindrops. Make a mobile to display the words.

 Number

Theme   Shape matching

Materials   Mastercopy 10

Method   Count how many there are of each shape. Colour the shapes in, one colour for each sort of shape. Match the shapes in the picture to the shapes round the border.

 General Studies

Theme   Shapes in nature

Method   Ensure that the children know how to do a rubbing before taking them outside. Try to choose natural things that have a definite shape. If it is not possible to go outside bring in some bark or leaves or find things in the classroom.

 Art and Craft

Theme   Shape pictures

Method   You will need large templates of a fish, an octopus, a tortoise and a hedgehog. The children can either draw or cut out the shapes to go in each creature. They put semi-circles in the fish, circles in the octopus, squares in the tortoise and triangles in the hedgehog.

Physical Education

Theme   Shape mats

Method   Have some simple shapes cut out to place on mats scattered round the hall. The children move around and on a signal (make the shape in the air to see if they are looking) they move to the correct shape mat as quickly (and safely!) as possible. The last one on the mat and any children who go to the wrong mat are out.

 Movement and Drama

Theme   Body shapes

Method
1. Get the children to make odd shapes using different parts of their body. They can all think of heads, arms and legs, but what about elbows, ankles and wrists? Look at the shapes and see if they can explore different levels, twists, arches, curls and stretches.
2. Using the sound of a tambourine helps during the creation of different shapes as it gives the children a set time to move. Let them work in pairs choosing their favourite shape to see if their partner can copy exactly. Try and find words to express the shapes the children make – if you can't find a word, make one up!

LOWER JUNIORS

 Written Work and Language

Theme   Speech marks

Method   Written conversation/speech has a definite shape. Revise speech marks with the children to ensure that their knowledge is accurate. Give the children two simple titles and let them work in pairs to make up the conversation orally before writing it down. It will be very helpful if the teacher joins in this activity – perhaps you could start the lesson off by holding a conversation with one child.
1. 'Why are you late for school?'
2. 'What did you do at school today?'

 Number

Theme   Shapes from shapes

Materials   Mastercopy 32

Method
1. Let the children cut out the square and divide it into the marked pieces. From these seven pieces they can make a triangle, a rectangle and a parallelogram. What irregular shapes can be made by rearranging the pieces?
2. Fractions of shapes; explore how different shapes can be divided equally and what the fractions of these shapes are called.

 General Studies

Theme   Cloud shapes

Materials   Mastercopy 33

Method   Clouds are condensed water vapour. They form when moist air is cooled either by wind moving the air over sea to land where it must rise and cool, or when cold air meets warm air causing the warm air to rise and form clouds, or when air currents rise from hot land cooling with ascent to higher altitudes.

Clouds have definite shapes and are signs of weather. How many can the children identify without seeing any pictures? You can then show them the Mastercopy.
Use these interesting cloud facts:-
1. Cumulus clouds may be formed by heat rising from forest fires.
2. A tornado is a spinning funnel of cloud extending from the base of a cumulo-nimbus. If it reaches the ground it is the most destructive of storms.
3. A cloud seven miles high can be seen from a distance of 240 miles. It then appears just on the horizon.

 Art and Craft

Theme 1   Three-dimensional shapes

Materials   Coloured paper cut into shapes of varying sizes

Method   Divide plane shapes by folding and leaving folded areas to provide a 3-D effect; also by folding and cutting. Use these shapes to make patterns on a contrasting colour of paper.

Theme 2   Circle mobiles

Materials   Paper, scissors, thread

Method   Cut a large circle and decorate it. Mark two smaller concentric circles in the large circle and cut them out too. Trim a fine edge away from the inner circles. Place them concentrically – there should be a space between the circles. Glue thread to the centre of the smallest circle and across the other two rings so that the circle mobile can hang and spin freely.

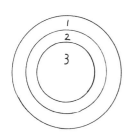 

 Physical Education

Theme   Shape activities

Method   The children can practise different activities linked to shape that warm the body before more exhausting P.E. activities.
1. Stretching –large and wide⎫ ⎧symmetrical
            large and thin ⎭ ⎩assymmetrical
2. Curled shapes extending to twists and arches
3. Stepping –large slow steps⎫ ⎧simple and intricate pathways
            small quick steps⎭ ⎩different directions

 Movement and Drama

Theme   Repetitive machine movements

Method   Divide the class into three or four groups and let them work out

repetitive, automatic movements. Stress that these types of movements have definite start and finish places, rhythm and effort. Suggest movements that might help e.g. pressing, rolling, punching, wringing. The class is going to make a machine that makes something. Perhaps it would help to decide on the end-product before the machine gets going. Let the children create the machine with body movements, flowing from one group to another to represent the manufacturing processes.

UPPER JUNIORS

 Written Work and Language

Theme   Creative writing in a given or chosen shape

Method
1. Let the children draw the shape and cut it out. Use it as an inspiration for written work. For example, if a child cuts out a cat shape the writing should be about cats. Suggest that the shapes are kept simple e.g. house, flower, train. The writing should follow the shape of its outer shape.
2. Explain that writing can form a picture of the subject matter by the way it is written down. A shape poem about a river can follow the path of a river, meandering all over the page.

 Number

Theme   Hexagon problem

Materials   Mastercopy 34

Method   Cut out all the hexagons carefully. Place them with one in the centre and six round the outside. But each side that touches another must make a total of 10. Here is the centre hexagon as a starting point in case you get desperate!

Theme   Measuring and estimating angles

Materials   Mastercopy 35

Method   Use the Mastercopy for work on angles. Take this opportunity to remind the children of right-angles, 180° on a straight line and 360° round a point.

 General Studies

Theme   Shapes in nature – vegetable cell

Method   All parts of plants are made up of cells. These cells are so tiny usually that they can be seen properly only under a microscope. They are what makes a plant a living thing because they feed, grow, reproduce and die.
Cells look like tiny compartments fitted together and they can be found in a variety of shapes – oval, polygonal, spherical, crescent-shaped, cylindrical to name a few. Each cell is made up of the same things structurally. A cell wall of thin membrane surrounds the protoplasm which is made up of cytoplasm and a nucleus. Let the children make simple diagrams to show that they understand this structure.

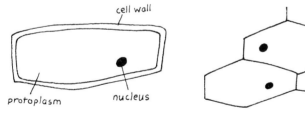

Further work can be to look at vegetable cells more closely and find out about endoplasm and ectoplasm, plastids and vacuoles. An important comparison is the one between vegetable cells and animal cells; vegetable cells have a firm cellulose wall and animal cells do not.

 Art and Craft

Theme 1   Printing with shapes

Materials   Empty matchboxes, cardboard tubes, cotton reels are good natural shapes to use for printing.

Method   Let the children be inventive in their pattern design. Start with design sheets where they can try out a number of ideas. Choose the best one and use it to print the cover for a note book.

Theme 2   Tessellation

Method   A tessellating shape is one that can be repeated without leaving spaces between the shapes e.g. an equilateral triangle will tesselate but a circle will not. Let the children make patterns with basic shapes before experimenting with more complex tessellation. Use of colour can greatly enhance the patterns.
Some shapes that tessellate:-

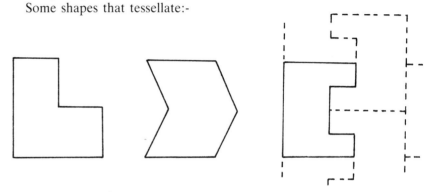

Theme 3   Positive/negative

Materials   A piece of white paper and a piece of black paper half the size of the white

Method   Cut a shape from the edge of the black paper and lay it in position on the white. These designs can become more complex as the children understand the concept involved and begin to be more experimental in their work.

 Physical Education

Theme   Musical shapes

Method   Divide the class into groups. Use some music, or if that is not possible, decide on a type of movement to be used. On a given signal and oral direction, the groups must make the shape you call. Award points for inventiveness and accuracy.

 **Movement and Drama**

Theme   Relationships

Method
1. Working individually, the children adopt different shapes. Question whether they are pointed or rounded, small or large. Is the emphasis high or low? Get the children to make one shape that includes one of each of these criteria.
2. Work in pairs so that one partner grows into a shape and the other mirrors it and becomes linked to it. The second then moves into their shape and the partner mirrors and links to that. This will need work and possibly adjustment of original shapes.
3. Work in threes – use the same method as with the groups of two but then the third member becomes a third dimension of the shape. Ask the children how this alters the body shapes and relationships.

QUICKIES

1. Answer the following questions to test your knowledge.
   a. How many sides has a circle?
   b. How many sides has an octagon?
   c. How many sides has a pentagon?
   d. How many edges has a 20 pence piece?
   e. How many edges has a 50 pence piece?
2. What shape are the following dwellings? Can you draw them and write underneath who lives in them?
   a. a wigwam   b. an igloo
3. Answer these questions:-
   a. What is the sum of all the numbers in the circle?
   b. What is the sum of the numbers in the circle only?
   c. What is the sum of the numbers in the triangle?
   d. What is the sum of numbers in the triangle only?
   e. What number appears in the circle and the triangle?

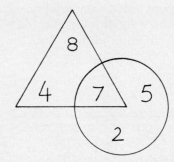

4. Subtract each triangular number from the square number above it. Can you see a pattern in the sequence of answers?
   square number: 1   4   9   16   25   36   49   64
   triangular number: 1   3   6   10   15   21   28   36

16 CIRCLES

INFANTS

 Written Work and Language

Theme   Writing practice

Method   Stress the sound of the letter being used.

1.

Joining shapes at the top – check that the letter is being formed correctly.

2.

This is good for pattern-making and size discrimination.

 Number

Theme   Exploring a circle

Materials   Pre-cut circles, crayons

Important words   Circumference, radius, diameter

Method
1. Give the children two circles each. Point out the circumference, radius and diameter. Fold the first circle in half across the diameter and colour one half. Fold the second circle in half and then in half again. This gives the radius and also shows one quarter. Open out the circle, colour one quarter and point out that the fraction left uncoloured is three quarters or a half and a quarter. These circles can be mounted and used attractively for display.
2. The activity can be extended to work on a clock face. Use it to reinforce o'clock, half past, a quarter past and a quarter to.

 **General Studies**

Theme 1   Useful and playful circles

Method   Get the children to look for circles around the classroom. See if they can collect any circular objects. Gather all the objects and sort them into useful or playful circles. See if they can think of any more circles outside the classroom (roundabouts, hoops, the big wheel). Ask them to draw pictures of the things they have thought of and decide into which category they fall.

Theme 2   Wheels are circles

Method   Find pictures of as many things as you can that move on wheels. Fill in the gaps from your own knowledge. Discuss the size, number needed, materials they are made from. Make a frieze of as many wheels as you can find.

 Art and Craft

Theme 1   Printing with circle shapes

Materials   Cardboard tubes, straws, bobbins

Theme 2   Bubble pictures

Method   Use paint mixed with washing-up liquid in an empty margarine pot. Blow down a straw into the paint and when the bubbles form, gently press a piece of paper onto the bubbles. When you remove it, you will find that the paper has a bubble print on it. (See also on page 57.)

Physical Education

Theme   Musical mats

Method   Space large mats around the room in a circle. Play some music and get the children to move in a circle over the mats. Change the types of movement and direction but when the music stops anyone who is on a mat is out.

Movement and Drama

Theme   Circle songs and games

Method   Use any of the following songs and games to reinforce the circular theme.
1. Ring-a-ring-o'-roses
2. The farmer's in his den
3. There was a Princess long ago
4. I sent a letter to my love
5. In and out the windows
6. Hokey-Cokey
7. My small ring
8. Allygaloo
9. Here we go round the Mulberry bush
10. Here comes Mrs Macaroni

LOWER JUNIORS

 Written Work and Language

Theme 1   Spelling

Method   At the beginning of the day write a list of words on a piece of paper that can be pinned up somewhere obvious in the room. The children should be warned that they may or may not know how to spell the words. They will be tested on them last thing in the afternoon. (Remember to leave time for this!)

open   orange   outline   ooze   onion
ocean   octopus   oil   oxygen   orbit

Theme 2   Shape writing

Method   Give each child a cut-out circle 8 or 9 inches (20–22 cm) in diameter. Write a story in spiral either starting from the outside or the middle. Give the children the title 'The Runaway Balloon'. When finished mount the circles as hot-air balloons – attach them with a paper fastener so that they can be turned round to be read. Draw in the ropes and basket.

 Number

Theme   Relating decimals to money

Method   Start off by going over place value. Give the children some numbers and ask them to identify the hundreds, tens and units. If they are quite sure of this, introduce the decimal point and explain that the figures to the right of the point become part of the whole – tenths, hundredths. Set up a table to show how amounts of money can fit into the scheme.

Give the children amounts of money in pence and ask them to write them in on their own table. Stress that the unit they are working with is £1 so 150 pence becomes £1.50.

 General Studies

Theme   Circles

Method   Circles and rings have long been held as having magic powers. This superstition arose from the belief that magicians had the power of imprisoning demons in rings. Ask the children to research some of the following circle topics:- The Magic Circle, fairy circles, Stonehenge, origins of the word 'circus'.

 Art and Craft

Theme 1   Spirals

Method   Give the children a circle of coloured paper. Draw a spiral on it and follow the line to cut. Any decorating should be done before cutting.

Theme 2   O-shaped faces

Method   Use a circular base shape – add all the features but each must be a circle.

 Physical Education

Theme   Hand rounders

Method   This is rounders played with a tennis ball but no bats. The batsmen must use their hands to hit the ball. Divide the class into two teams and set out a rounders pitch with four posts.
Rules:
1. A player can be out at any post.
2. You are out at first post only if the ball is hit behind.
3. Score one point for each post passed but only on your own go.

 Movement and Drama

Theme   Pathways, levels, relationships

Materials   As many shakers as you can find

Method   Practise moving in various pathways (curved, straight); walk them, run them. Add leaping to the travelling and after the leap, freeze the landing position. As a class co-ordinate a step-hop-hop pattern in a circle. Get uniform rhythms then increase the speed. Freeze movements periodically. Try again using shakers as an accompaniment. Set up a dance idea:-
1. An Indian chief calls his tribe into a circle by using his shaker.
2. Tribal dance (step-hop-hop)
3. Indians place their shakers in a circle and repeat the dance faster and faster. Stop.
4. Slowly pick up shakers and then in own time run, leap, scream (if you can stand it!), freeze; do this three times.
5. Chief calls tribe into spiralling group until it is in a tight circle crouched near the floor.
6. Slowly rise together, turn together, run, leap, (scream), freeze together.

UPPER JUNIORS

 Written Work and Language

Theme   Story-writing

Materials   Dictionaries if available

Method   Ask the children to write a story using as many 'o' words as they can. The story should be no longer than 150 words and will score one point for every word beginning with an 'o' that is correctly used and spelt.

 Number

Theme   Decimals

Method
1. Make the largest and smallest number that you can using all four digits:-
   5   2   7   1   9   8   0   9

2. Make the largest and smallest number that you can using all four digits and a decimal point within the digits:
   2   5   3   7   4   0   0   4

3. Arrange in order starting with the smallest number:-
   a. 3.03,   30.3   0.303   303
   b. 5.22,   5,   5.2,   5.02,   5.022,   5.002
   c. 4.612,   46.2   4.62   0.462   2.162   46.12

4. 45.61   62.78   14.97
    21.36 +   19.13 +   36.56 +
    _____   _____   _____

    _____   _____   _____

5. 74.53 _   54.56 _   41.75 _
    12.21   22.35   19.87
    _____   _____   _____

    _____   _____   _____

6. 36.43   11.27   24.32
    × 3   × 4   × 5
    _____   _____   _____

    _____   _____   _____

7. 48.36 ÷ 3   62.75 ÷ 5   21.74 ÷ 2

 **General Studies**

Theme　　Wheels

Method　　Before the invention of the wheel, travellers walked or rode on animals carrying their own luggage. The next step was to pull the luggage along on a branch or to make a simple kind of sledge. It was found easier to move heavy things on rollers e.g. logs. The children can experiment with this method of transport using pencils. The first wheels were very heavy because they were made from solid wood. Gradually the hole in the middle of the wheel became larger ending up with spokes and rims. Rubber tyres filled with air made travelling in wheeled vehicles more comfortable.

1. Can the children think of any other uses of the wheel?
2. How did civilisation benefit from the invention of the wheel?

 Art and Craft

Theme 1　　Simple masks

Method　　Use a sugar paper circle for the face which is cut out and decorated. Cut a one inch (2.5 cm) wide band from stiffer paper or card and glue or staple the mask on to it at the front.

Theme 2　　Making owl-like birds

Method　　Cut out a circle and then cut it in half. Overlap the semi-circles so that the straight edge is on the outside. Stick them together. Add eyes, ears, feet and feathers made from tissue paper.

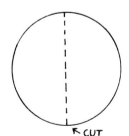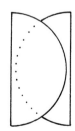

 Physical Education

Theme　　Wandering ball

Method　　Form the children into a circle with one or more in the middle. Throw a ball or beanbag across the circle from player to player. Those in the centre try to intercept the passes. If they are successful they change places with the thrower.

 Movement and Drama

Theme　　Poetry

Materials　　'The Bear Hunt' below

Method
1. Get the children to sit in a circle while they are learning the words and actions.
2. Start beating a rhythm with hands on knees. Return to this rhythm between actions.

The Bear Hunt
I want to go on a bear hunt
All right! Let's go!　*(Beckoning gesture)*
Oh look! There's a brook
Can't go round it
Can't go under it
Can't go over it
Got to go through it　*(Hands together fish-tail movement)*
All right! Let's go!　*(Beckoning gesture)*
Oh look! There's a bridge
Can't go round it
Can't go under it
Can't go through it
Got to go over it　*(Over an arch shape)*
All right! Let's go!　*(Beckoning gesture)*
Oh look! There's a swamp
Can't go round/under/over it
Got to go through it　*(Slow rhythm making sucking sounds)*
All right! Let's go!　*(Beckoning gesture)*
Oh look! There's a tree
Can't go round/under/over/through it
Got to go up it　*(Climbing hand over hand)*
All right etc.
Oh look! There's a cave
Let's go and see what's inside　*(Peering as though separating greenery)*

All right etc.

Let's go softly. Let's go quietly   *(Change rhythm)*

Oh look! I see two big eyes   *(Fingers circle round eyes)*

I see two big paws   *(Hold up paws)*

I feel something like a fur coat   *(Stroke arms)*

It looks like a bear. It feels like a bear.

It is a bear!   *(Hands spread in surprise)*

Let's go! Up the tree. Down the tree.

Through the swamp   *(Repeat all appropriate gestures)*

Over the bridge

Swim the brook

Down the street

Open the gate. In the door. Shut it fast.

Phewwwwwwwwwwwwwwww   (Wipe brow)

Bernice Wells Carson

David R Ginglend

QUICKIES

1. Sit the children in a circle and give them each a number. The teacher starts off.
   Teacher: 'The Prince of Wales has lost his tails and number 1 knows where to find them.'
   The replies go like this:
   Number 1: 'Who sir, me sir?'
   Teacher: 'Yes sir, you sir'
   Number 1: 'No sir, not I sir. It's number 4 sir'
   Number 4 then takes up with 'Who sir, me sir?' and the game carries on. If anyone fails to give the right answer then they must pay a forfeit and start the game again.

2. Collective nouns are the names given to groups of things.
   What is the collective noun for:-
   a.   a number of singers
   b.   a number of fish
   c.   a number of geese
   d.   a number of musicians
   e.   a number of eggs

3. Here are the signs of the Zodiac. Can you match them to their correct meanings?

Signs		Meanings	
Aries	Libra	bull	ram
Taurus	Scorpio	fishes	virgin
Gemini	Sagittarius	crab	lion
Cancer	Capricorn	water-bearer	scales
Leo	Aquarius	goat	scorpion
Virgo	Pisces	twins	archer

17 COLOURS

INFANTS

 Written Work and Language

Theme   Acting on oral instructions

Materials   Mastercopy 36, story below

Method   Use the Mastercopy as a picture for each child to colour. Read the story that gives the colours and matches the picture. Then let the children complete the colouring on their own.

The Rainbow

It had stopped raining and the grass in the garden looked very green. The oak tree with its big brown trunk and new green leaves stood dripping water on the yellow daffodils underneath.
The children stood by the red front door. Keith had on his black wellingtons and new blue mackintosh. Mary had red wellingtons and a yellow mackintosh. They were just about to run down the path to the gate when Keith said, 'Oh look, Mary! It's a rainbow!'
'Where?' said Mary.
'Over there above the oak tree.' said Keith.
And sure enough there was the most beautiful rainbow of red, orange, yellow, green, blue and purple stripes that they had ever seen.

 Number

Theme   Matching and sorting

Materials   Buttons, cotton reels, beads, bricks; circles of basic colours large enough to collect on

Method   Spread out the coloured circles and ask the children to sort out the chosen materials to the correct colour-matching circle. Divide into groups and let the children grade each colour group according to shade or size of object.

 General Studies

Theme   Primary and secondary colours

Materials   Paint and paper

Method   Check that the children know the primary colours. Experiment with mixing colours to get the secondary colours. This can be done effectively by making a triangle with coloured dots and joining the dots with lines to a central colour point.

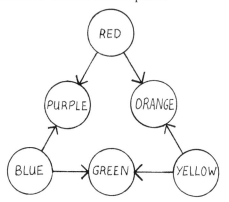

 Art and Craft

Theme 1   Drip painting

Method   Use straws dipped in colours and then dripped on to a contrasting background.

Theme 2   Stained-glass window effect

Method   Spread PVA adhesive onto a piece of polythene (cut from a polythene bag). Tear small pieces of coloured tissue paper and place them on the adhesive so there are no gaps between – the pieces will overlap. Cover this with a layer of watered-down adhesive and leave it to dry. When it is dry you can peel the polythene away from the tissue leaving a stained-glass window effect which can be mounted in a frame.

Theme 3   Illustrate the poem 'Piles of Golden Oranges' on page 79

Piles of Golden Oranges

Piles of golden oranges,
Grapes both black and green,
Pyramids of apples
And the largest plums you've seen.
Earthy brown potatoes,
Cauliflowers and sprouts,
People push and jostle
Everybody shouts.

Stalls are getting empty,
Barrows wheeled away,
Have we bought enough to last
Until next market day?

Marcia Armitage

 Physical Education

Theme 1   Relay races concentrating on balance

Method   Give each team a colour name and bands for identification if possible.
1. Balance beanbags on heads
2. Balance a small ball on flat open palm
3. Balance on heels and move backwards
4. Step with heels touching toes (fairy footsteps)

Theme 2   Play 'Farmer, farmer, may I cross your golden river?'

Method   One child is the farmer, the rest of the children are at the other end of the hall. Children ask 'Farmer, farmer, may I cross your golden river' (the large space in the middle of the hall). The farmer says 'Only if you are wearing . . . . . .' (chooses a colour). All children wearing that colour must try and get to the other side of 'the river' (the other end of the hall) without being touched.

 Movement and Drama

Theme   Colourful people and movement

Method   One of the places where we find most colour is in the circus.

Talk about this with the children and find out how much they know. Create a ring by seating the children. The teacher is the Ring Master; have fun with the class making up the acts.

LOWER JUNIORS

 Written Work and Language

Theme   Descriptive writing

Method   Explain to the children that there are sometimes easy ways of remembering facts. One of these is to remember the colours of the rainbow with the word VIBGYOR – Violet, Indigo, Blue, Green, Yellow, Orange and Red. Vibgyor is a Rainbow Man. Ask the children to write about him and describe him:

1. What he wears
2. Where he lives
3. What he likes to eat
4. What his hobbies are.

 Number

Theme   Multiplication

Method
1. Colour code the numbers from 0 to 9 (red, yellow, green, blue, black, orange, purple, grey, brown, pink). Make sure the children have or can see a copy of the code.
2. Choose any multiplication table in need of practice and make a diagram of the table. Nine times table and five times table are particularly good because they have such a definite number pattern. Each time a number is written it must be the right colour. Stipulate that the arrow means multiply.

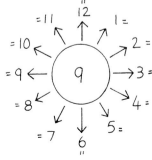

General Studies

Theme   Colour chemistry

Method   Remind the children how recent the use of colour is. Most of them will have seen black-and-white films on television and perhaps some of them realise that not all television sets are colour models! There are also black-and-white photographs. What other things do we take for granted – coloured clothes, cars, food?

Where did colour originate? Natural colourants include onion skins, flowers, roots. Some colours were difficult to produce hence purple, being the most important rare colour, was used for the Roman rulers' clothes. Early oil paintings show that the artists used many methods to create colour.

Where is colour most important? – safety signs, traffic lights, electrical wiring.

 Art and Craft

Theme   Shades and blends of colour

Method
1. Each child chooses one colour of paint. Using a plain piece of paper they start at the top and paint a stripe of pale colour. Add a little more powder paint to deepen the colour and paint another stripe. Continue until the page shows bands of graded shade from light to dark. Use this paper as a background for a cut-out silhouette.
2. A similar idea to above but this time choose three colours and blend the bands of colour to give a background related to a theme:
   a. Fireworks – red, blue, yellow
   b. Sunset – red, orange, yellow
   c. Spring – green, blue, yellow
   Add one or more appropriate silhouettes to the picture to finish it off.

 Physical Education

Theme   Three and over

Method   Divide the class into two teams of twelve. The playing area should be the length of the hall divided into two with a goal for each half. Space out the teams on either side of the centre line. 1 passes the ball to 2 who passes to 3. Then the ball must be passed over the line

to 4; he passes to 5 who passes to 6 who can then score a goal by placing the ball in a hoop. The scoring team must stand still when they have the ball. Only the opposition can move to intercept a pass, but when they get the ball they must stand still and pass to the next player in their line. When a goal is scored the first pass is given to alternate teams. Players 7–12 start out as defending members of their teams. Both teams play simultaneously.

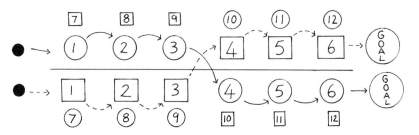

 Movement and Drama

Theme   Market traders

Method
1. Discuss the different stalls that you might see on a market and the different selling techniques that the traders use. Is the best sales pitch the most flamboyant?
2. Allow the children to choose whether they want to be stall-holders or shoppers. Let them work out their own ideas then choose the best and elaborate on them to create a market atmosphere.

UPPER JUNIORS

 Written Work and Language

Theme   Dictionary work leading to imaginative writing

Materials   Dictionaries

Method
1. Ask the children if they know the names of any colours that you find in a paint box. Any paint tins in the art area will provide the same information. Colours have descriptive names to show different shades

of colour e.g. vermillion, carmine. Using the dictionary see if you can make a class list of as many names as possible.

2. Suggest some written work that can involve the different colour names – describing a picture, designing clothes, a story with as many colours in as possible.

 Number

Theme 1   Factors

Materials   Mastercopy 6 (100 square)

Method   Use the hundred-square Mastercopy with the border. Leaving the top left-hand corner square empty, put the numbers 1–10 across the top and 10–100 (in tens) down the side. The children must find the factors for each number down the left-hand side and mark them in on the grid. Choose a colour code before you start (see Lower Junior section on Number on page 79).

	1	2	3	4	5.	6	7	8	9	10
10		■		■						
20		■	■							■
30		■	■		■					
40		■		■	■			■		

Theme 2   Tables

Materials   Mastercopy 6 (100 square)

Method   Use the Mastercopy as a hundred square without the border. This work can be done on squared paper, as ideally each table needs a fresh hundred square. Agree a colour code for each table e.g. 2x – red, 3x – blue. The children mark in the table on each hundred square by colouring the appropriate number squares.

 General Studies

Theme   Light

Method

1. We normally think of light as being white but there are actually many different colours. Sir Isaac Newton first defined the seven colours that make up white light – red, orange, yellow, green, blue, indigo and violet. The colour we see depends on the wave-length of light that strikes our eyes. When light rays fall on any surface they penetrate a little into the substance, are partly absorbed and partly sent back in all directions, or *reflected*. The sensation of colour is created by the wave-length of light which is reflected.

   a. An orange skin will absorb all colours except yellow, orange and red which are reflected back.

   b. An object appears black when it absorbs all the light and reflects nothing.

   c. White objects reflect all colours – all colours mixed together make white light.

2. The children can make a colour spinner. You will need a circle of card divided into six segments. Colour the segments red, orange, yellow, green, blue and purple on both sides of the card. Make two holes in the centre of the circle and thread through some fine string, shirring elastic or wool to make a loop about half a metre long. To use the spinner, hold the two ends of the string almost taut and spin the disc round until the string is twisted. Jerk in the opposite direction and the disc will spin round. What happens to the colours?

 Art and Craft

Theme 1   Colour combinations

Method   Using two chalk crayons or pastels draw two bands of colour and then blend the colours with your finger to make a new tone in the centre. This can be done several times with different combinations of colour to create new effects. When the experimental work has been done, use these colour combinations in a picture. A drawing of an exotic bird or flower makes good use of this technique.

Theme 2   Shooting stars

Method   The children draw a cross on their paper and then add two or more diagonals. Each pair of lines is joined by an oval at the top. Colour in the oval and then decorate each cone shape by any means. Cut out the shape leaving a border of white all round (this also saves the children cutting too close to the centre). Mount the work on black paper and cut it out again, this time leaving a black border. The work can now be mounted on any colour paper for display.

 Physical Education

Theme   Traffic lights

Method
1. Divide the class into two teams with either the teacher or a spare child as 'traffic controller', who stands at the far end of the room, back to the rest. The teams line up at the opposite end ready to move up their own 'road'.
2. The controller shouts 'green' and the players hop towards him or her.. On the call 'amber' the players proceed with caution on all fours. When 'amber' has been called, the controller turns round, points to a team and shouts 'red'. All players in that team must freeze and not move. The controller can call 'red' to the other team or turn back again, call 'amber' followed by 'green' (without turning) or 'red' again turning and pointing to one team.

    Anyone caught not obeying the signal is out, likewise anyone who moves on 'red'. The controllers must follow the correct colour sequence of lights but they can vary the period of each colour. The winner is the first person to reach the controller and becomes the next controller.

 Movement and Drama

Theme   Effects of colour

Method
1. More and more research is being done into the effect different colours have on people – whether beneficial, stimulating, relaxing etc. See what the children feel about colours. Some suggestions are red – exciting; blue – cool, calm; green – relaxing; orange – warm; beige – restful; yellow – bright, stimulating.
2. Can the children relate their feelings into movement, mime or drama? Let them work in groups and use each other as an audience.

QUICKIES

1. Read this test to the class and see how alert they are:
    1. Put your first and last name on the bottom right-hand corner of your paper
    2. Draw a circle round your first name
    3. Draw a triangle in the centre of your paper
    4. Draw a square around the triangle
    5. Turn your paper over
    6. Write your initials in the upper left-hand corner of your paper
    7. Use a red pencil or crayon and draw a long line on the left-hand side of the page
    8. Use a green pencil or crayon and draw a short line at the bottom of the page
    9. If you didn't have the correct coloured crayons or pencils put a yellow square round your initials
    10. If you didn't have a yellow pencil or crayon make a wavy line down the right-hand side of your paper.
2. What is:
    a. a white lie
    b. the White Ensign
    c. the white flag
    d. the White House
    e. a white-out

18 LETTERS

INFANTS

 Written Work and Language

Theme   Vowels and consonants

Materials   Mastercopies 37–39

Method
1. Introduce the work by going through the alphabet to point out that the letters fall into two groups – vowels and consonants. If a word begins with a consonant it has 'a' before it but if it begins with a vowel it must have 'an'. Write up some examples.
2. To make a team game, divide the class into five groups and let each group represent one vowel. Each member of the team has to provide
   a.   a word beginning with their vowel
   b.   a word with their vowel in it.
3. The Mastercopies can be used for colouring. Pupils can be asked to produce their own ideas for x and z.

 Number

Theme   Big and small

Method
1. How many letters can the children find that will fit inside themselves to make one big and one small?

2. See if there are any children in the class whose names begin with the same initial e.g. Clare and Catherine.
3. Is one of the children bigger than the other? This will lead to a comparison of size.

 General Studies

Theme   Simple symmetry

Materials   Mirror, cards with upper-case letters printed clearly

Method
1. Explain the meaning of symmetry. Let the children experiment with the mirror and cards to see how many letters they can find which look the same upside down or can be seen to be the same when a mirror is held at right-angles to the card. Explain that some letters are symmetrical when cut in half. Find these by putting the mirror in the middle of the letter either vertically or horizontally
2. To illustrate this symmetry, the children can draw the letter with each matching half in a different colour.

 Art and Craft

Theme   Letter shapes

Method 1   Potato prints can be done with letter shapes but they do need to be prepared beforehand.

Method 2   Draw a large letter for each child with a thick crayon or felt-tip pen. See if they can add more to make the letter into something – preferably something that begins with that letter.

Method 3   For this activity you will need scrap pieces of coloured sugar paper and alphabet templates. Get the children to cut out the letters of their name. With a needle and thread (the teacher's job) join the letters together to make a name mobile.

Physical Education

Theme   Team game to reinforce vowel names

Materials   Hoops, beanbags

Method   Divide the class into five teams named a, e, i, o and u. Stand them behind a line and place two hoops with beanbags in them at intervals from the line. The first member of each team has to run out and collect the beanbags without touching the hoops. They give them to the second members of their teams who replace them in the hoops and run back to touch the third members of their teams, who are then free to run out and collect the beanbags and so on down the team. The first team to finish must all sit down in the right order and shout out their vowel name.

 Movement and Drama

Theme   Phonic pairs

Method   The children illustrate in movement the contrast between the pairs of words. There are some examples given here. We have made the contrast between weak and strong movements.

mighty mouse	meek mouse
loud lion	lazy lion
wicked witch	weary witch

LOWER JUNIORS

 Written Work and Language

Theme   Letter writing; capital letters and punctuation

Materials   Mastercopy 40

Method
1. Show the children how to set out a letter and how to address an envelope. Ask them to write and thank a relation for sending them something they didn't really want or already had. The main point of the letter is that it must cause no offence to the sender.
2. Use the Mastercopy as an exercise in punctuation and setting out a letter.

 Number

Theme   Sorting into sets

Method   Look at all the letters of the alphabet and sort them into four sets – open letters, closed letters, curved letters, straight letters. Are there any that fit into more than one set? How can we show this? (See Venn diagrams on page 15–16.)

 General Studies

Theme   The beginning of the alphabet

Method
1. The Phoenicians were the greatest sailors of the Ancient World. The carrying trade was in their hands. They found the picture writing and wedge-shaped writing of the East too difficult for general use. They made a series of characters, which we call 'letters', which could be put together to make words. The Greeks copied these and made a few more. The Romans learnt from the Greeks and made more changes themselves. They gave us the 26 letters which form our modern alphabet. (This is the factual story of our modern alphabet.)
2. For a purely fictional (but very logical) view, use 'How the First Alphabet Was Made' from the *Just-So Stories* by Rudyard Kipling.
3. Use Mastercopies 37–39 to show a picture alphabet. The children can use this or make up some letters of their own to send a message to a friend.

 Art and Craft

Theme   Letter patterns

Method 1   Using letters of all shapes and sizes cut from magazines and newspapers make a pattern or form them into new words.

Method 2   Try writing your own name in different forms. If you were a designer could you design a label or trademark from your own name? Remember, it has got to be eye-catching and memorable.

 Physical Education

Theme   Circle relay

Method   For this you will need four teams, A, B, C, D, and beanbags. Arrange the teams as shown in the diagram.

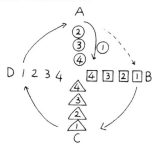

Number 1 from each team runs clockwise round the circle (all at the same time) and back into the place of number 4 of his or her team – while they are running the team should have moved up so number 2 is in the starting position. Number 1 passes the beanbag along the line to 2 who runs round and back to the end position. The relay finishes when the team is back in its starting position. It is a good idea to mark the starting place for each team otherwise the circle can get out of shape.

 Movement and Drama

Theme   Small group work

Method   This work can be linked to the Number section on page 84. Group the children in threes and fours. Remembering the general shape of various letters, get the children to explore through movement the character of group shapes:- wedge, square, globe, half-moon. Relate these to letter shapes. Each group shape will have a definite character (attacking, defending, ritualistic, encompassing). If the children associate their shape with a specific letter, let them use the phonic sound to heighten the dramatic effect of the movements created.

UPPER JUNIORS

 Written Work and Language

Theme   Alliteration

Method   Explain the word 'alliteration' and show how effective the use of it can be in prose and poetry.
1. One good example is this poem about Cardinal Wolsey:-

> Begot by butchers, but by bishops bred
> How high his Honour holds his haughty head.

2. In 1828, a certain Reverend B. Poulter composed a famous alliterative alphabetic poem in rhymes. Each word of each line begins with the letter of the alphabet it represents. We reproduce the first four lines.

> 'An Austrian army awfully arrayed,
> Boldly by battery besieged Belgrade;
> Cossack commanders, cannonading come,
> Dealing destruction's devastating doom; . . .'

Now follow that!

 Number

Theme 1   To find the lines of symmetry in all the letters of the alphabet

Method   Refresh the children's memory by going over the concept of symmetry. Remind them that lines of symmetry can be drawn vertically, horizontally and diagonally.

Theme 2   Seven-segment display

Method   Digital watches and clocks and calculators display numerals in a 'seven segment display'. This can either be with liquid crystals (LCD) or light emitting diodes (LED). Ask the children with digital watches if they have looked to see how the numbers are displayed. Using squared paper ask the children to work out the display format for the numbers 0–9. Each number is allocated two squares – one above the other (seven lines)

0123456789

 General Studies

Theme   Early writing

Materials   Encyclopaedia, *How Writing Began* 'Macdonald Starter Book' from the Long Ago series.

Method   Words were first conveyed from one person to another by means of pictures. From using a general picture to describe an event(a), man developed a picture for each word(b). The pictures below say 'I killed five sheep'

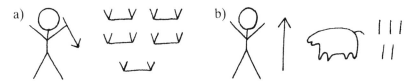

Pictures were drawn on the walls of caves and the Egyptians developed a picture writing known as hieroglyphics. Information on this can be found in most children's encyclopaedias. The trouble with this picture language was too many words and it took a long time to communicate an idea or message. First letters were sound pictures that could be drawn quickly and simply.

 Art and Craft

Theme 1   Illuminated letters

Method   It will help to give the children an idea if you can find some examples of this kind of work. Let the children choose a word and then illuminate the first letter in relation to the meaning of the word.

Theme 2   To design a logo

Method   Ask the children to design a company logo or personal stamp using just the initials of their name.

 Physical Education

Theme   Three-cornered netball

Method   Hoops are set out thus:

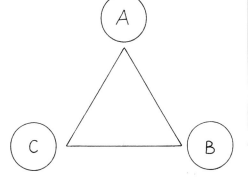

Arrange the children into three teams A, B and C and number the members of each team. The teacher calls out two numbers and the children involved have to pass the ball between them as in netball and then score in one of the other two goals while defending their own e.g. Team A can only score in the hoop of team B or C.
Rules:
1. There must be three passes before scoring.
2. The ball must be placed in the hoop to score.
3. Only overhead passes are allowed – no bouncing.

 Movement and Drama

Theme   Symmetry/Asymmetry

Method   Having worked on this theme in the Number Section (page 85), relate it to the body and note how it affects movement.
1. Symmetry – stable, balanced, solemn
2. Asymmetry – unbalanced, travelling, turning, free

QUICKIES

1. Find the different countries in these scrambled letters:-
    a. N S A I P
    b. R C N A F E
    c. D R L I A E D N
    d. G E P Y T
    e. R A S U L T I L A A
    f. G B L U M I E
    g. A N D C A A
    h. L I C E H
    i. D P L A N O
    j. B I T T E
2. Write a noun for each letter of the alphabet. Remember, a noun is the name of a person, place or thing.
3. Play *Bottles*. Start counting at 1 but every time you reach a number that has a 7 in it or is a multiple of 7 the person whose turn it is must say 'bottles'. If they say the number instead of 'bottles' they are out! It may be easier to start with 5 and multiples of 5 until the children get used to the idea of the game.

19 NEWSPAPERS

INFANTS

 Written Work and Language

Theme   Format and content of newspapers

Materials   A selection of current newspapers

Method
1. First find out how many of the children know if they have a newspaper delivered to their homes or if one of their parents buys one on the way to work and brings it home at the end of the day. Try to find as many names of newspapers as the children can give you and discuss why they are so named – *Times, Telegraph, Observer, Mirror*. See if the children have any ideas as to what kind of varied information is contained in a newspaper – not only news but weather, television programmes, star charts, letters.
2. An obvious extension of this is to make a class paper with an appropriate title but this activity obviously takes quite a bit of time.

 Number

Theme   Working with money

Material   Mastercopy 41

Method   Use the Mastercopy as a money-matching exercise. If you can find any plastic or cardboard money in the classroom let the children use it practically to make up the amounts in as many ways as possible.

 General Studies

Theme   Where do newspapers come from?

Method   Give the children this question to think about. See if they can work it out for themselves but be ready to fill in any knowledge gaps. This may mean that it takes a while to get to the pulp stage, but encourage positive logical thought.

Paper in house – paper shop – printers – paper manufacturer – pulp mill – tree-felling – tree.

 Art and Craft

Theme   Paper-tearing

Materials   Newspaper, glue, sticky tape, rubber bands. A helpful book is *The Art of Paper Tearing* by Eric Hawkesworth (Faber and Faber).

Method 1   To make a tree – stick four sheets end to end. Roll them up and secure with a rubber band. Make three cuts along the tube to half the tube length. Pull out from the centre.

Method 2   To make a ladder – roll the paper up as above, but mark into thirds, cut out two-thirds of the central section, bend back outer thirds to make bottom rung. Pull out from centre.

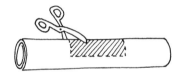

1. cut out shaded section

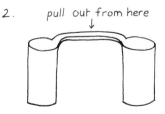

2. pull out from here

end sections bent back

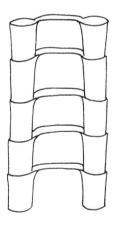

3. "expanded" ladder

Physical Education

Theme   Games with newspapers

Method 1   Variation on 'I sent a letter to my love' using a rolled up newspaper to drop behind the chosen person.

Method 2   Cut out fairly large fish shapes from newspaper. Form teams and have a relay race flapping the fish along the floor with a folded paper up to a line and back again.

 Movement and Drama

Theme   Make a newspaper in dance

Method   Split up the action into:
1. Felling the tree – pushing and pulling
2. Rolling the logs – bending and rocking
3. Pulping the wood – rhythmic
4. Pressing the sheets – pressing
5. Typing the news – short, sharp tapping
6. Setting the print – slow and delicate
7. Rolling the presses – fast, circular
8. Folding the paper – precise, linear
9. Selling the paper – expansive gesturing
10. Reading the paper – straightforward mime
    Decide on the different work actions as a class and practise as a class. Separate into groups for each action and then start the action at felling. All movements must keep going until the 'paper' is read.

LOWER JUNIORS

 Written Work and Language

Theme   'Can the camera lie?'

Materials   Variety of large pictures cut from newspapers

Method   Give the children a picture each or between two and ask them to write the story that they think might have accompanied that picture. If you have kept a record of the events covered by the pictures, a comparison can be made with the stories that the children have written.

 Number

Theme   Making a block graph

Materials   Pages of a newspaper that list that day's television programmes

Method   Each child has a piece of paper on which he puts the four television channels into columns across the top. Down the side he puts times in half hours from noon to 10 pm. Using the television programme schedule provided, he must list the programmes that he would watch between those times with continuous viewing. Explain that as some programmes overlap, care should be taken to allow for this. When the schedule is completed the children then add up the time used for viewing on each channel and make a block graph to show how they used the time given.

 General Studies

Theme   Conservation

Method   Make the statement that newspapers are made from trees. Can any of the children tell you how? A tree takes far longer to grow than a paper takes to be read and thrown away. This makes a newspaper seem very extravagant in terms of growth and time.

    Recycling is becoming increasingly important because we cannot afford to lose all our trees before they can be replaced. Ask the children to think of how many ways paper can be recycled. How can we save paper? We can re-use envelopes, buy recycled note-paper and carrier bags.

 Art and Craft

Theme   To colour-code using newsprint

Materials   If possible felt-tip pens, if not good crayons

Method
1. Colour words in the newspaper to alphabetise – all words beginning

with 'a' colour red, those beginning with 'b' colour green and so on.

2. Block out the paragraphs with primary colours. Either of these two ideas can then be cut from the paper and mounted to make a multi-coloured print collage.

 Physical Education

Theme   Stationary relay

Method   Children sit in a line. Use a rolled-up newspaper for the 'baton'. The baton can only be passed to the next person if they say the correct word. If they cannot think of a word in the group being used at the time, then they are out. Some suggestions for groups are dogs' names, car names, flower names, pop groups.

 Movement and Drama

Theme   Mime

Method   Mime a scene from a favourite television show. The mime must be silent! The rest guess which show.

UPPER JUNIORS

 Written Work and Language

Theme   Story and letter writing

Method
1. Give the children some 'Historical Headlines' and let them write the story as it might have been reported in a newspaper of the time.
   a. 'Drake plays bowls as Spaniards sail by'
   b. 'Raleigh puts cloak in puddle'
   c. 'Cordon Bleu Alfred?'
   d. 'King hides in oak tree'
   We had great fun thinking of these headlines so perhaps the children might like to make up lists of their own.
2. Write a letter to the Editor of a paper either to complain about school, leisure facilities in your area, a national or international event or in praise of them.

 Number

Theme   Direction finding

Method
1. First of all make sure that the children know the eight basic points of the compass. Ask them to draw and label them.
2. The map below shows the position of four paper boys and girls. In which direction will each child have to walk:
   a. To collect his or her money from the paper shop?
   b. Then to go on home for breakfast?

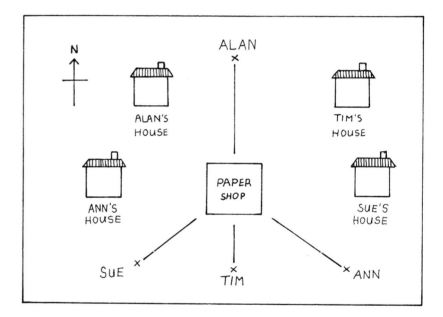

 General Studies

Theme   Printing

Materials   *Printing Processes*, (Ladybird) 'How It Works' Series, No. 13

Method   The newspaper as we know it would not have existed without sophisticated printing techniques. The earliest form of print was invented by Johannes Gutenberg in Germany in 1455. The earliest English print was produced by William Caxton in Flanders in 1476. He then moved back to London and produced the *Canterbury Tales* by Geoffrey Chaucer in 1478. His methods of printing were used for many years, all sheets being printed by hand. Newspapers used this handmade method until the nineteenth century at which time the men who printed *The Times* could turn out only 250 sheets per hour. Ask the children to do some research into modern printing methods. See what they can find out about new computerised systems.

 Art and Craft

Theme 1   To make a picture using newsprint

Method
1. Choose one word in fairly large print from a newspaper. Cut it out and stick it in the middle of a sheet of paper. Then draw the word as many times as you like, but each time although using uniform letters, the size and shape of the word must change.

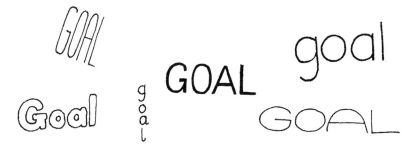

2. Use cut-out letters to make a simple picture.

Theme 2   To make 'magic bangles'

Method   Make three cuts to halfway down a piece of paper the size of a large newspaper. Stick the first strip to the other side to make a loop. Give the second strip a twist before sticking to the other side to make a loop. Give the third strip two twists before sticking to the other side to make a loop. Continue cutting the strips to form three bracelets. Cut each bracelet in half around its circumference – you should then have two identical bracelets, one large necklace and one pair of handcuffs!

 Physical Education

Theme   'Deliver the newspaper'

Method   Roll up and secure a sheet of newspaper into a javelin shape. You will need one 'javelin' for each member of the team. Depending on space available have either two or four teams playing at once. Line the teams up behind a drawn line with the appropriate number of baskets or waste bins at a suitable distance from them. The idea is for each member of the team to 'deliver' the newspaper from behind the line and then move to the back of the team. When all papers are successfully delivered, the team can sit down.

 Movement and Drama

Theme   To explore the role of advertisements

Method   This activity will need some discussion on the role of advertising in newspapers and magazines. Does it work? Why does it work? Divide the children so that they can work in groups. Give each group a product to advertise e.g. toothpaste, food, car etc. The group must then make a short advertisement which has the essential elements of movement and music and/or sound. They are limited to using five words only because the more words used the longer it takes.

QUICKIES

1. Explain the following words–
   newsagent   newscast   newsletter
   newsreel   newsprint   news-stand
2. Take a column of newsprint. Look for words starting with vowels. Gather five words beginning with each of the vowels. If you don't know what it means – look it up!
3. One-minute interviews BUT the interviewee must not answer the questions with 'Yes', 'No' or 'I don't know'! Anyone who does not last the minute is out.

20 COMMUNICATION

INFANTS

 Written Work and Language

Theme　Spoken communication

Materials　Story such as *The Surprise Party* by Pat Hutchins

Method
1. Read the story to the children. Play a game to show how spoken communication can go wrong. Sit round in a circle with a slight space between each child. The teacher starts by whispering a message to the nearest child. This child passes it on to the next and so on round the circle. You will be very surprised if the last child repeats exactly the same message that was given at the beginning.
2. Ask the children how many ways we can use our voices to communicate – talk, shout, whisper, sing, order. Get the children to try each method. Which do they like best?
3. Choose five children to say the same words to the class but each must use a different method to say:
   "Please will you all sit down and be quiet"
   Which one did the class like best?

 Number

Theme　Listening

Materials　Each child will need a piece of paper, pencil, crayons and counters.

Method
1. As you read out the description of the number picture, the children draw it and colour it afterwards.
   Draw a big house with three windows and a front door.
   Draw one tree in the garden with two birds sitting in it.
   Draw two children playing with their parents. What are they doing?

2. Give the children five counters each. The teacher gives sums by tapping instead of saying the numbers. Let the children use the counters to aid accuracy.

 General Studies

Theme　Posting a letter

Method
1. Do the children know what happens to a letter after it is put into the post-box or before it arrives through the letter-box? Take them through the various stages that a letter must take on its journey from one person to another.
2. Perhaps they could write a letter and post it to the teacher's address. Then she could send a reply.

 Art and Craft

Theme　Communication pictures

Method　Give the children a simple circle shape to be filled in with an original picture. Make it a face that is communicating some emotion. Refer to the Infant Written Work and Language section in Signs, Symbols and Signals on page 64.

 Physical Education

Theme　Circle game

Method　Get the children to form a circle with two children in the centre. Give two players on opposite sides of the circle a beanbag each. They put the beanbag behind their backs and on the first signal pass it round the circle behind their backs. On the second signal the passing stops and the children in the middle have to guess who is holding the beanbag. If they guess correctly they change places with the one who was holding it. If not they must stay in the centre for another go.

 Movement and Drama

Theme　Laughing

Method   Laughing can be one of the easiest ways of communicating. Set up the situation so that the children can find the difference between laughing with someone and laughing at someone. Hopefully they will all decide that the former is best!

1. Things that make us laugh at someone:-
   a. People tripping over
   b. When someone has a new haircut
   c. When people can't do something
   d. When someone doesn't understand an instruction or makes a mistake
2. Things that make us laugh with someone:-
   a. Tickling
   b. Pulling funny faces
   c. Parties
   d. Trying to keep a straight face
   e. Funny jokes – someone is bound to know one!

LOWER JUNIORS

 Written Work and Language

Theme   Spoken communication

Method
1. Start with a discussion on man's need to communicate. This should lead to answers which fall roughly into separate headings e.g. worship, love, hunger, danger. How does man communicate these needs? The spoken word is the most obvious.
2. Give the class a task (either in groups or individually) to find words that may or may not be linked but which communicate expressively the ideas behind the chosen categories. The class can judge whether this task has been effectively completed or not.

 Number

Theme   Basic rules

Method   Write the four mathematical signs on the board and ask the children to write the correct word or words for each sign on their own paper. Check that all the answers are correct and add in any that may have been missed.

e.g. minus
      take away
      subtract
      find the difference between

      add
      total
      find the sum of

Give unanswered sums orally using all the different terms that have been written down.

 General Studies

Theme   Communication through the ages

Method   Ask the children to think of all the ways man has communicated important news through the years. See if you can make a class sequence pictorially with captions.

    Pyramid stones → Biblical decrees → Riders with messages → Town criers → Telegraph → Telephone → Computers →

 Art and Craft

Theme   To illustrate a poem

Materials   *The King's Breakfast* on page 93

Method   Use this as a class activity. Read the poem and let the children choose their own words and pictures to illustrate it as literally or humorously as they can. Drawing helps them to learn the poem and makes a recital at the end of the activity, holding up the pictures instead of saying all the words, much more fun.

Physical Education

Theme   Free Dodgeball

Materials   1 ball, a set of bands

Method   Two teams, one marked with bands. The 'bands' pass the ball to one another trying to hit the 'non-bands' below the knee. Anyone who is hit, joins the bands.

Rules
1. Only a hit below the knee counts
2. You are not allowed to run with the ball.
N.B. An enclosed space is necessary for this game.

 Movement and Drama

Theme 1   Charades

Method   Establish signs for book, TV, film, words, syllables, before play starts.

Theme 2   Non-verbal communication – body language
We can tell a lot about how people are feeling or what sort of people they are by the way they stand, sit and move.
1. Some body shapes are strong: symmetrical
2. Some body shapes are closed: unwelcoming, asymmetrical
3. Some body shapes are open: welcoming
A simple way of getting the children to experience all these is by sitting on a chair.
   a. Sit square, upright, symmetrical, feet flat on the floor, legs slightly apart.
   b. Same position but slump, put one hand to mouth.
   c. Same position as (a) but cross arms, head on one side.
   d. Same position as (a) but move both feet slightly to one side.
   e. Lean back in the chair and stretch out legs.
The combinations are endless and provide the beginning of many dramatic situations. A good start is to let one child sit in a certain way and get another to come in and question the person seated. The seated person does not reply in spoken language but can alter body shape to communicate a reply.

The King's Breakfast

The King asked
The Queen, and
The Queen asked
The Dairymaid:

"Could we have some butter for
The Royal slice of bread?"
The Queen asked
The Dairymaid,

The Dairymaid
Said, "Certainly,
I'll go and tell
The cow
Now
Before she goes to bed."
The Dairymaid
She curtsied,
And went and told
The Alderney:
"Don't forget the butter for
The Royal slice of bread."
The Alderney
Said sleepily:
"You'd better tell
His Majesty
That many people nowadays
Like marmalade
Instead."
The Dairymaid
Said, "Fancy!"
And went to
Her Majesty.
She curtsied to the Queen, and
She turned a little red:
"Excuse me,
Your Majesty,
For taking of
The liberty,
But marmalade is tasty, if
It's very
Thickly
Spread."
The Queen said
"Oh!"
And went to
His Majesty:
"Talking of the butter for
The Royal slice of bread,
Many people
Think that

Marmalade
Is nicer.
Would you like to try a little
Marmalade
Instead?"
The King said,
"Bother!"
And then he said,
"Oh, deary me!"
The King sobbed, "Oh, deary me!"
And went back to bed.
"Nobody,"
He whimpered,
"Could call me
A fussy man;
I only want
A little bit
Of butter for
My bread!"
The Queen said,
"There, there!"
And went to
The Dairymaid.
The Dairymaid
Said "There, there!"
And went to the shed.
The cow said
"There, there!
I didn't really
Mean it;
Here's milk for his porringer
And butter for his bread."
The Queen took
The butter
And brought it to
His Majesty;
The King said,
"Butter, eh?"
And bounced out of bed.
"Nobody," he said,
As he kissed her

Tenderly,
"Nobody," he said
As he slid down
The banisters,
"Nobody,
My darling

Could call me
A fussy man –
BUT
I do like a little bit of butter
to my bread!"

A. A. Milne

UPPER JUNIORS

 Written Work and Language

Theme   Communication and responsibility

Method   Discuss with the children how they feel about topical news subjects. Are they swayed by headlines? Are we numbed by too much communication (i.e. terrorism, famine). After the discussion ask the children to write their own comment. Is freedom of the press valuable?

 Number

Theme   Binary numbers

Method   The characters which a computer can store and process form the character set of that computer. Character code is a type of code where a group of binary digits (in this case four) is used to represent each character. The children can learn how to form the character code for the numbers 1–9. All they are doing is working in base 2 as opposed to base 10.

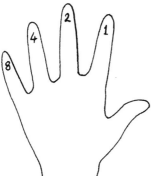

This is a number system which uses only the digits 1 and 0.

1. Base 2 or binary system
For number 1 – bend over the finger with 1 on it. Any finger bent over is represented by 1, the straight fingers by 0 therefore:
   1 is 0001, 2 is 0010, 3 is 0011 (bend over fingers 1 and 2), 4 is 0100, 5 is 0101, 6 is 0110, 7 is 0111, 8 is 1000, 9 is 1001

2. Binary coded decimal
If you code each digit of a decimal number separately, the binary code produced is called binary coded decimal.
   73 is 0111 (7) 0011 (3)
   594 is 0101 1001 0100
Given the diagram the children should be able to work out the binary numbers for themselves and then translate decimal numbers into binary coded decimal.

 General Studies

Theme   Recording and communicating information

Materials   Large glass dish, food colouring, water, candle, cork (storage jar top works well), glass jar that cork will fit easily inside, small building bricks

Method   Scientific experiments have to be communicated and each experiment has a special way of being written down.
1. Set up the experiment to show that a flame needs oxygen to burn.
   a. Put bricks in glass dish. Fill with coloured water.
   b. Float candle which is secured to cork. Light candle.
   c. Invert jar over candle, resting on bricks.
   The candle stays alight until the oxygen in the jar is used up. The water rises because outside pressure is forcing the water to take the place of the oxygen. Repeat the experiment so the children can see it clearly and answer any questions that may arise.
2. The children must now communicate the experiment in written form under the following headings:-Experiment Title, Diagram, Method, Result, Conclusion.
3. This could lead to a discussion on fire safety precautions.

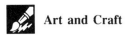 **Art and Craft**

Theme   Surrealism

Method
1. Use the concept of surrealist art as a starting point. Pictures by Dali or Klee and examples of modern advertising techniques can give the children some idea. Discuss this work with the children and see if they can express in picture collage the juxtaposition of ordinary objects. Let them work in pairs and if the work is successful, it can be extended to individual paintings.
2. If the children find this concept too difficult, suggest that they remember a dream they have had and try to draw a picture that communicates the dream.

 Physical Education

Theme   Moving target

Method   Two teams stand at each end of a divided space. Each child has two small balls or beanbags (one will do if there are not enough to go round). Put a large ball in the centre space between the two teams. Each team aims from behind their marked area with balls or beanbags. The object is to get the large ball over the opponent's line.

 Movement and Drama

Theme   Body shape

Method   The children work in pairs. Tell them that they are sculptors creating a sculpture that communicates something, such as anger, humour, panic, horror etc, using their partner's body.

QUICKIES

1. Learn this poem and then recite it – in one breath!

Farmer Jackson's Farm
Farmer Jackson has on his farm
One dog
Two cats
Three goats
Four pigs
Five hens
Six cows
Seven geese
Eight ducks
Nine sheep
Ten lambs
And hidden away where nobody sees
A hundred hundred honey bees.

Clive Sansom

2. In how many ways can you communicate the spoken word?
3. Design your personalised telephone – one that suits your personality!
4. From these clues work out the day's timetable. There are four lessons in the morning and four in the afternoon.

   a. English is the first lesson after lunch
   b. Geography is before Maths
   c. English is before French
   d. History comes between Science and French
   e. Biology is between Geography and Games

Mastercopy 1

Look at these shoes. Can you tell whether they were worn by men or women? Do you see a resemblance to any modern styles?

Chinese	Indian	Assyrian	Egyptian	Primitive
Medieval	Byzantine	Roman	Greek	Persian
17th Century	17th Century	16th Century	16th Century	14th Century
19th Century	19th Century	19th Century	18th Century	18th Century
1950	1936	1923	1910	1900
1984	1984	1980	1970	1960

How many objects can you remember?

Is there an object for each letter of the alphabet?

My eye

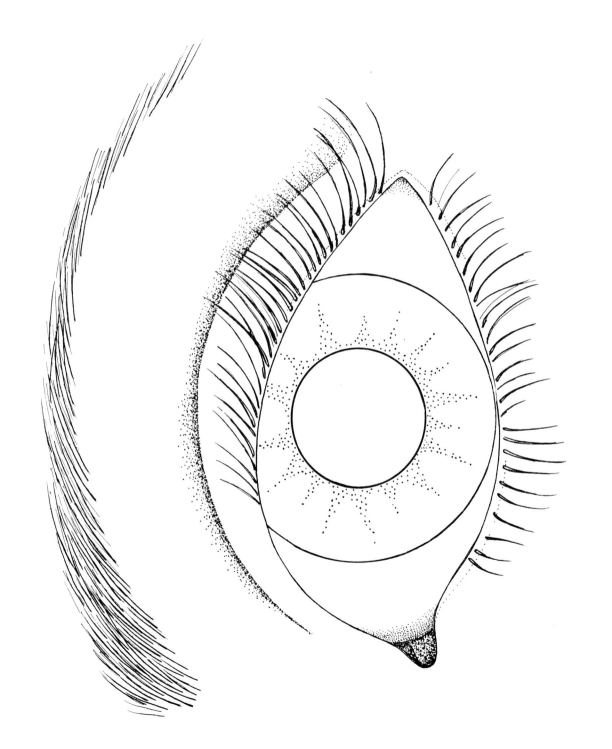

iris
cornea
pupil

brow
lid
lash

Find and label these parts of the eye.

rectus muscle   cornea   pupil   iris   lens   retina

optic nerve   blind spot

suspensory
ligament

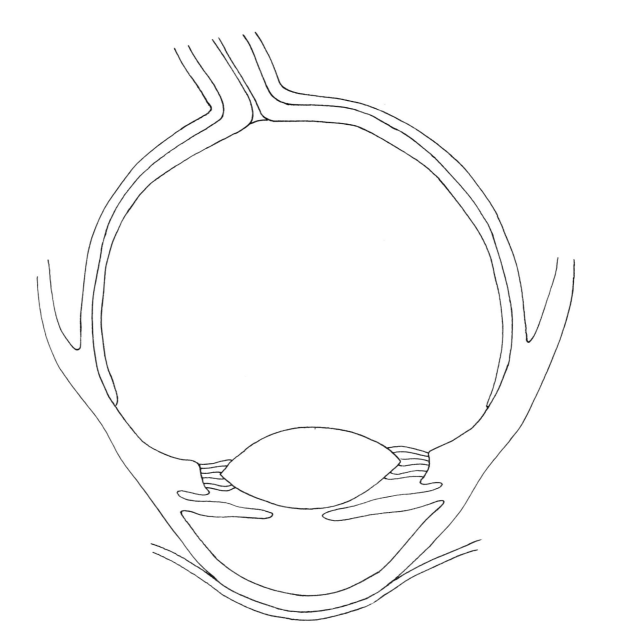

Section through the eye

Ask people what their preference is between the sweet and sour lists. Give a tick every time someone shows a preference.

Sweet

chocolate	
custard	
carrots	
ice cream	
parsnips	
bananas	
honey	
tomatoes	
cake	
cornflakes	

Total _____

Sour

cheese	
plain yogurt	
cucumber	
mayonnaise	
grapefruit	
marmite	
crisps	
lemon	
vinegar	
fish	

Total _____

Count up the ticks in each column.

Which do most people prefer – sweet or sour? ....

Mastercopy 6

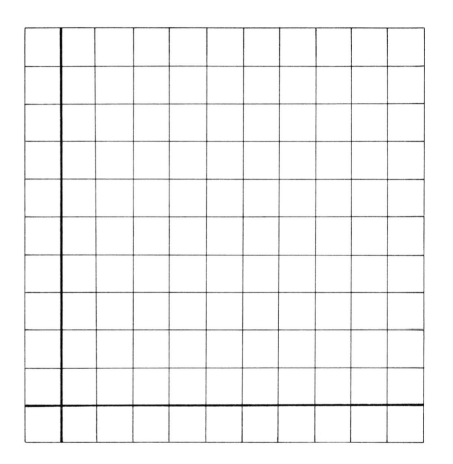

Match the hat to the person.
Do you know what each person is called?

Can you name these types of hat?
Try naming the country from which they come.

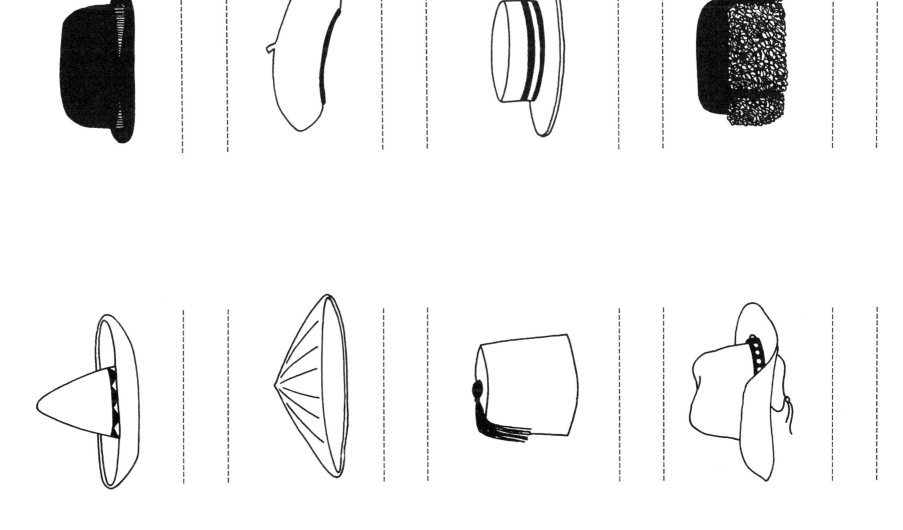

Measure the marked angles of each hat.

1.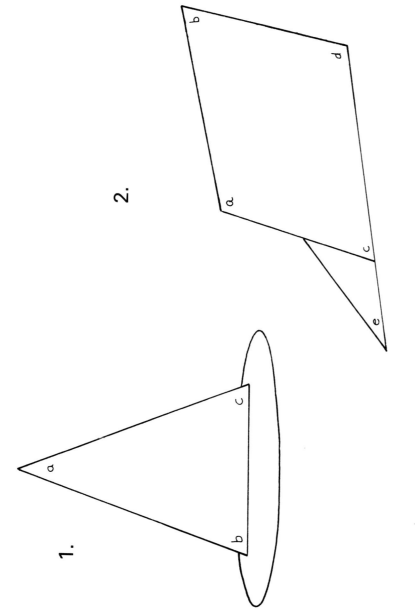

2.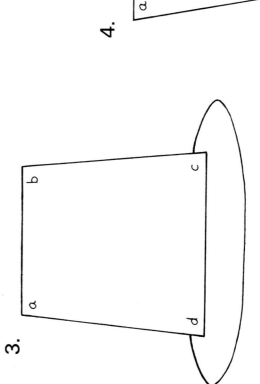

3.

4.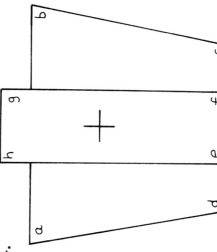

© Oliver & Boyd 1986

Mr. Shape is a robot. Colour him in. What are the names of the shapes from which he is made?

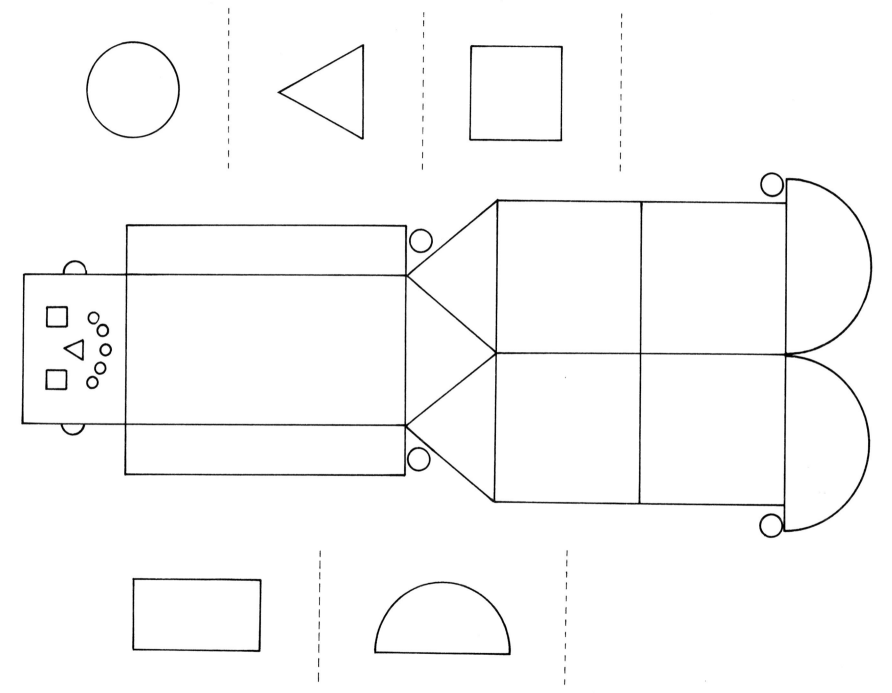

Here are some small creatures.
How many legs does each one have?

Spider

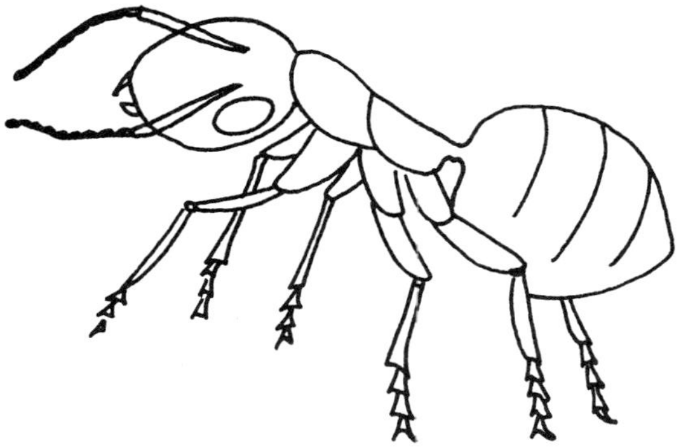

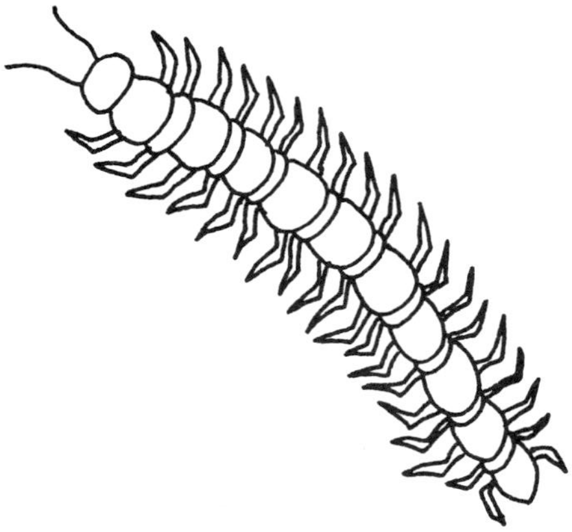

Centipede

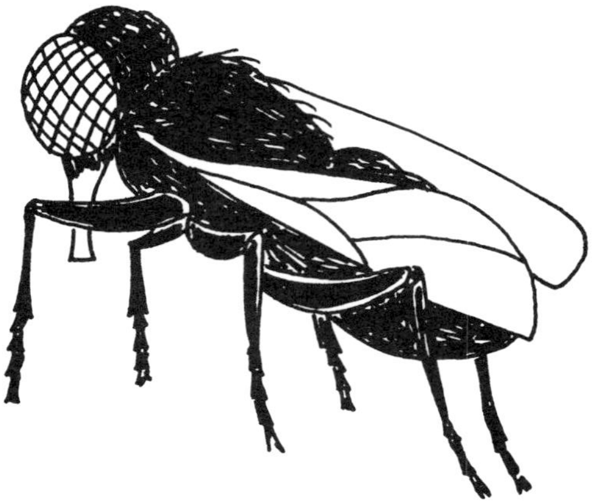

Fly

Ladybird

Ant

Woodlouse

Try to find your way to the centre of the maze.

Count and colour.

Colour and count.

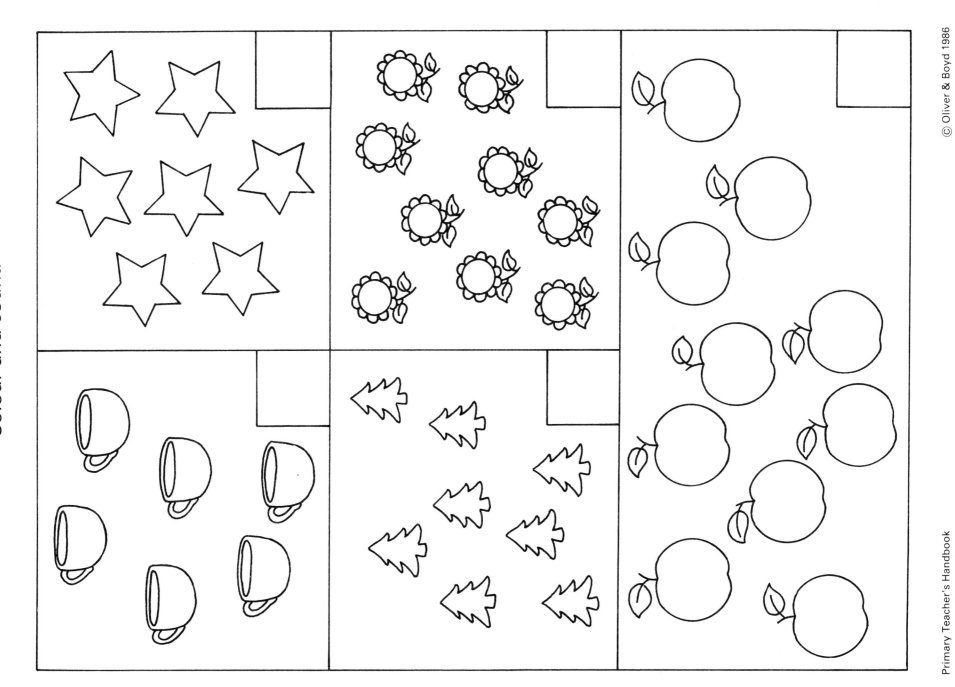

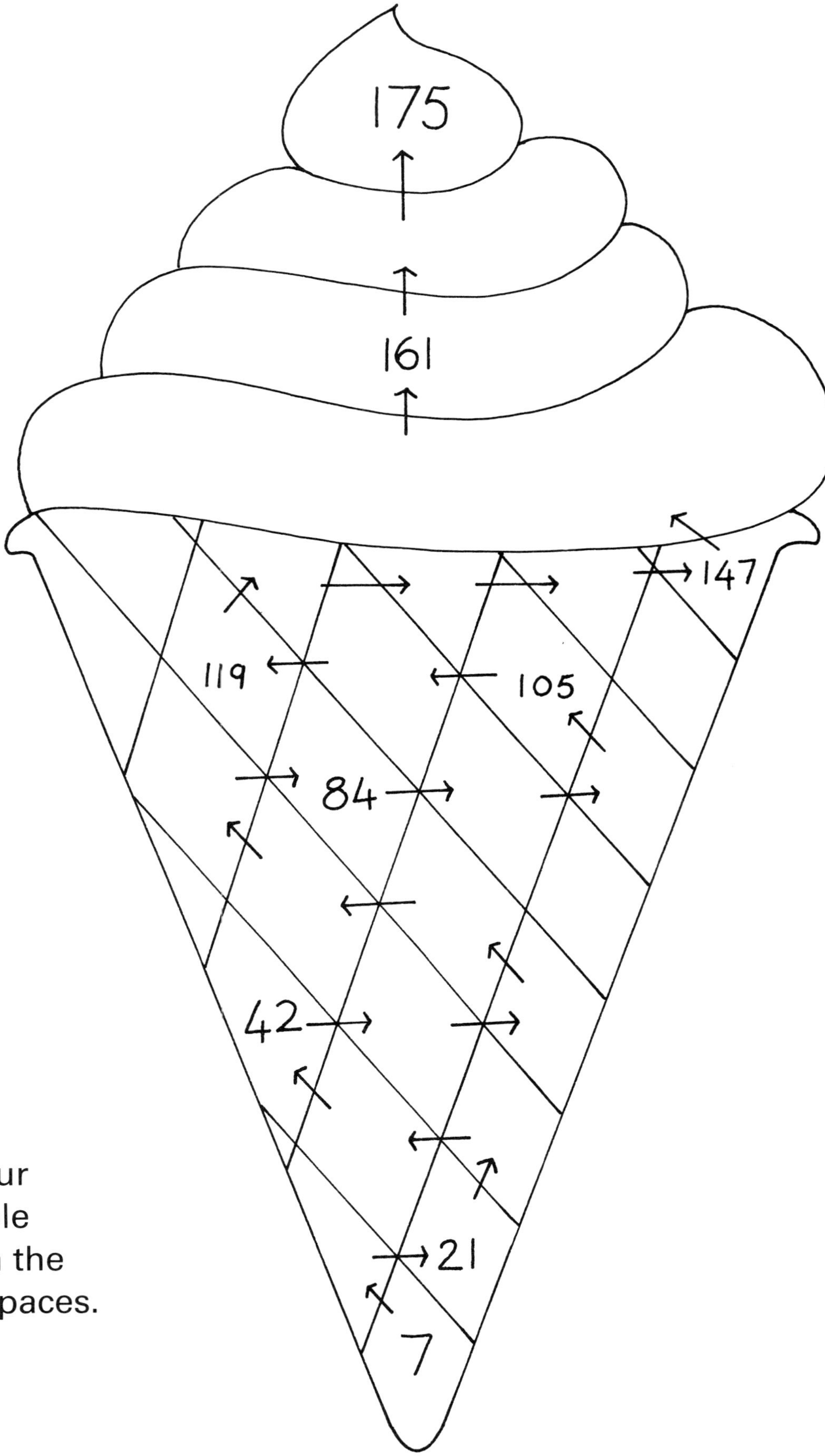

175

161

147

105

84

119

42

21

7

Use your
7 × table
to fill in the
blank spaces.

Find the answers.

11 × 8 =	13 × 3 =	5 × 3 =
40 + 27 =	13 + 80 =	3 × 7 =
6 × 6 =	11 × 3 =	12 × 8 =
25 + 6 =	76 − 8 =	11 × 5 =
40 + 17 =	100 − 9 =	12 × 7 =
54 − 7 =	56 − 3 =	9 × 8 =
80 + 18 =	9 × 6 =	53 − 10 =
3 × 10 =	19 + 10 =	5 × 5 =
8 × 8 =	7 × 11 =	7 × 10 =
6 × 8 =	3 × 4 =	4 × 4 =
10 × 5 =	90 − 8 =	32 + 62 =
32 − 10 =	7 × 8 =	40 + 33 =
9 × 7 =	60 + 27 =	9 × 9 =
10 × 9 =	90 − 11 =	10 + 27 =
10 + 9 =	20 + 6 =	70 − 9 =
6 + 5 =	4 × 10 =	18 + 60 =
40 + 6 =	81 − 10 =	32 + 6 =
4 × 8 =	26 + 32 =	75 + 8 =
7 × 5 =	11 × 4 =	12 × 5 =
20 + 14 =	66 + 8 =	10 × 8 =
100 − 3 =	30 + 21 =	9 × 11 =
30 + 11 =	5 × 9 =	46 + 46 =
5 × 4 =	19 × 5 =	10 × 10 =

Invent a colour key to explain photosynthesis.

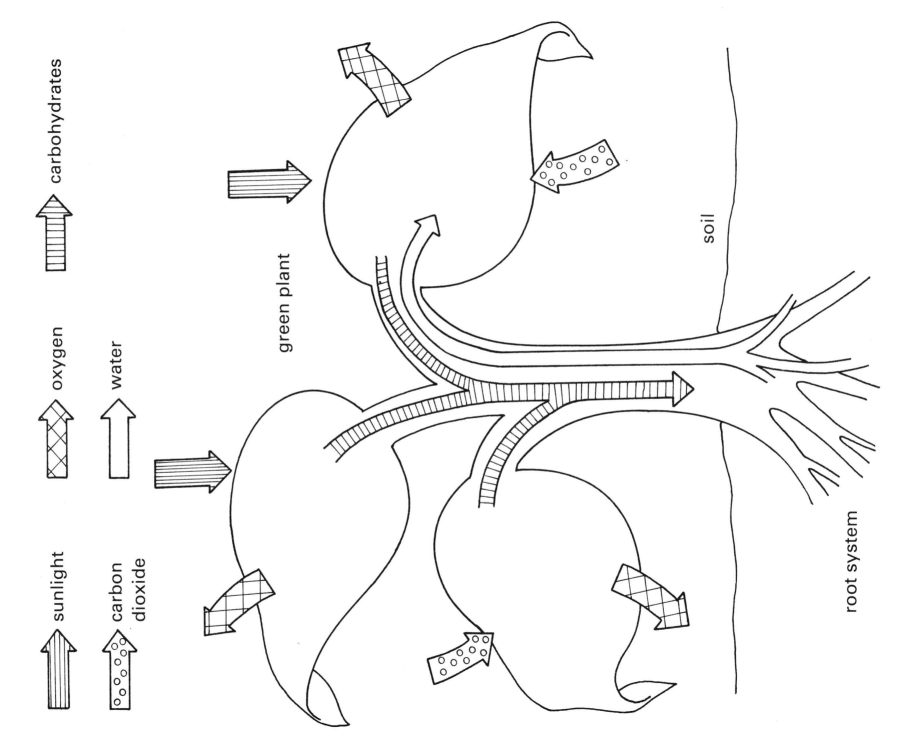

carbohydrates

oxygen

water

sunlight

carbon dioxide

green plant

soil

root system

Match the leaves. What are their names?

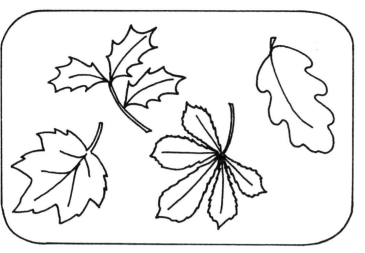

Here are the apple trees. The apples are in the baskets; from which number tree did they come? Match them up.

Read the passage and answer the questions by drawing a line under the right answers.

We often think of the potato as being a root. This is not so; it is a stem growing underground. In the spring tiny brown leaves begin to grow from it. I am sure you will all have seen the "eyes" of a potato, but do you know what they are? Each eye is a group of buds with a leaf just below them. When the shoots grow above the ground they turn a pale green. At first the shoot gets its food and water from the potato, but soon it grows roots which collect food and water from the soil.

1. The "eyes" of a potato

    (*help it to see/are a group of buds/are a group of stems*)

2. Underground potato leaves are

    (*green/black/brown*)

3. Pale green is

    (*a dark green/a light green/grey*)

4. A potato is a

    (*root/stem/shoot*)

5. At first the shoot gets its food from

    (*the eye/the ground/the potato*)

6. Often means

    (*many times/a few times/ always, never*)

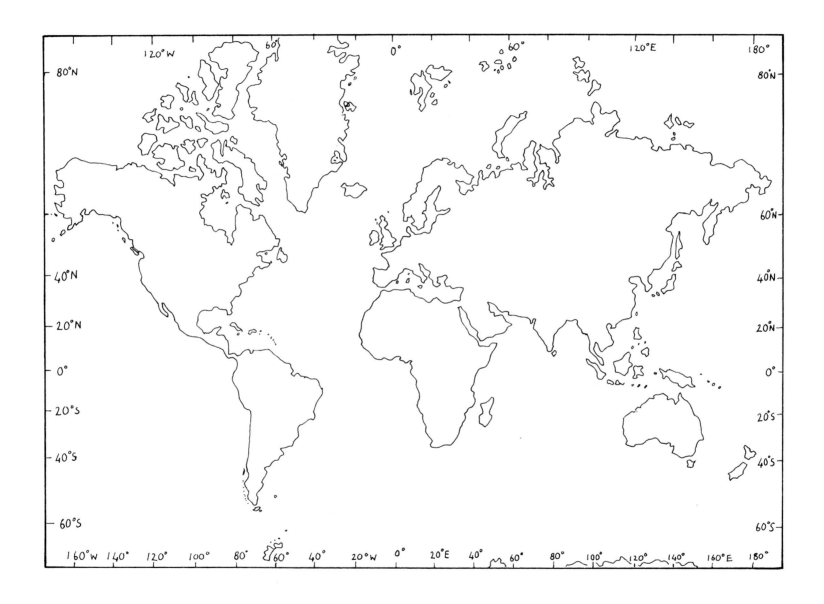

Colour the pictures.   Add up the sums.

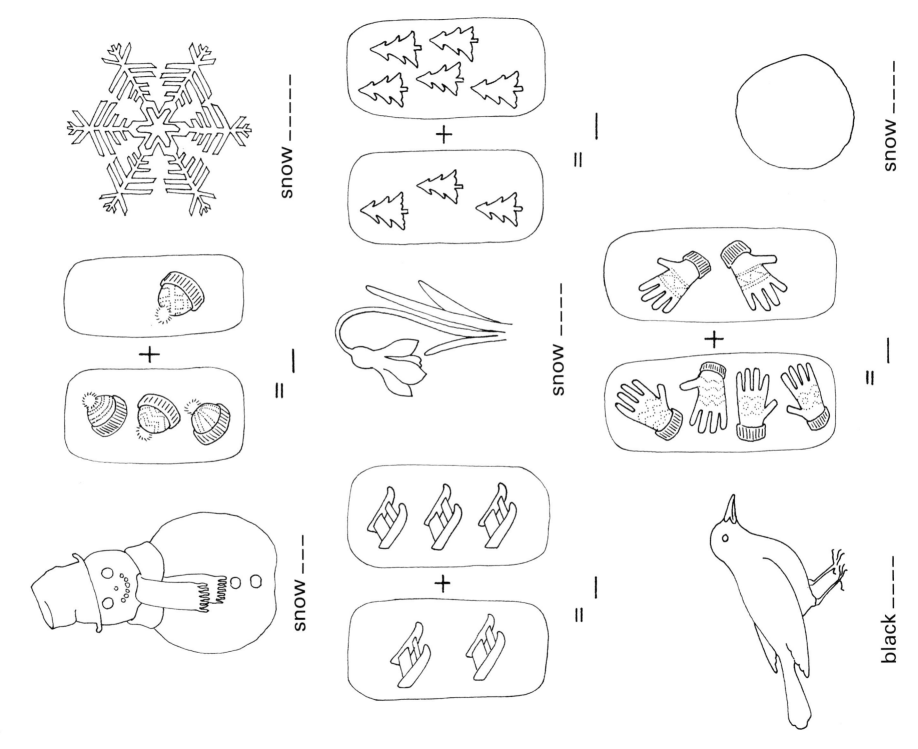

snow ____

+   =   snow ____

+   =   snow ____

+   =   ____

+   =   snow ____

+   =   snow ____

+   =   black ____

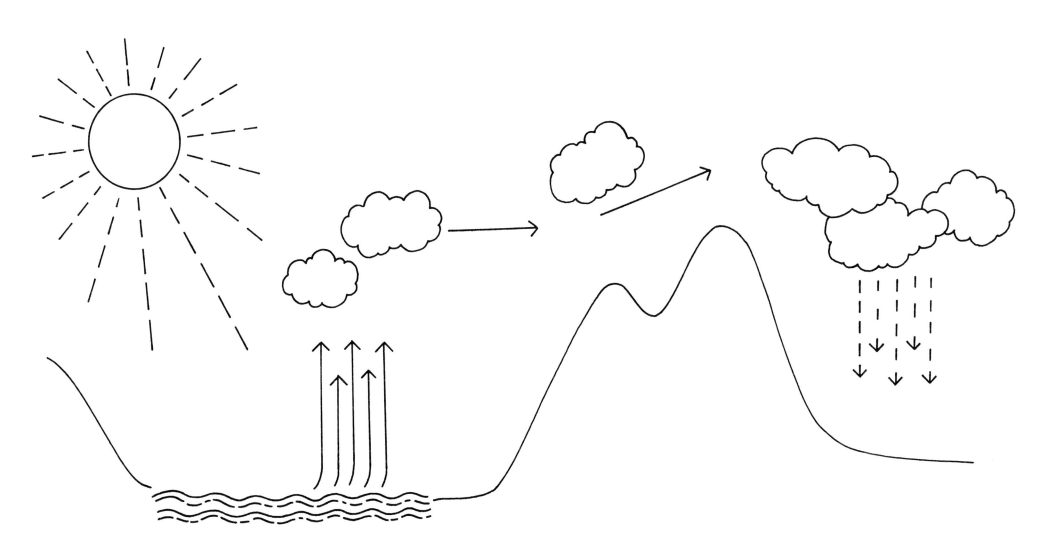

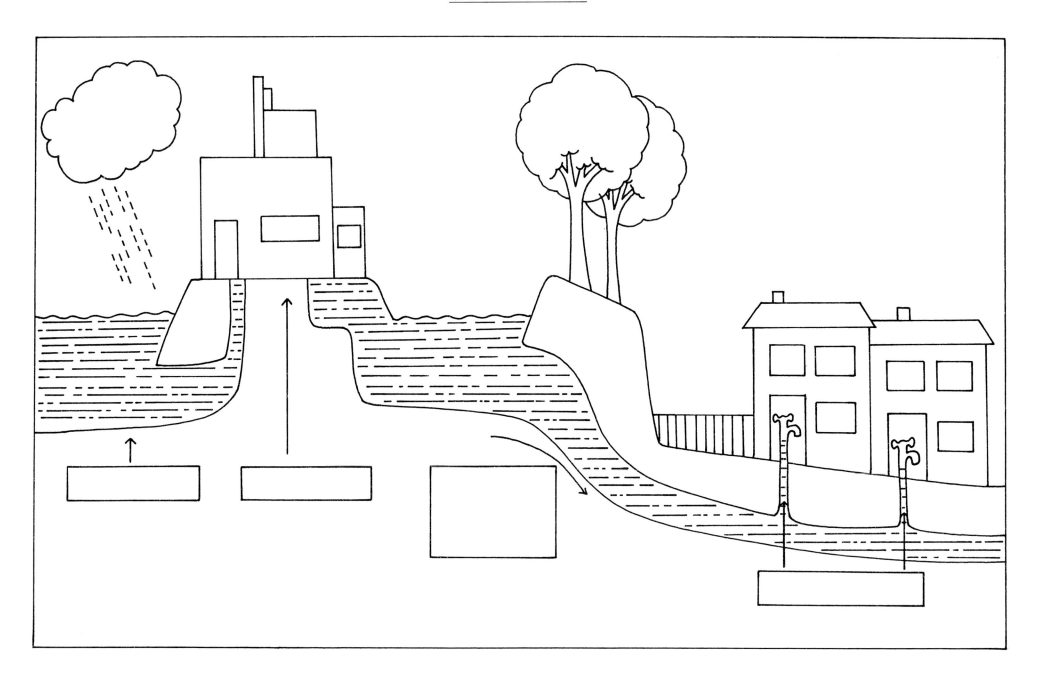

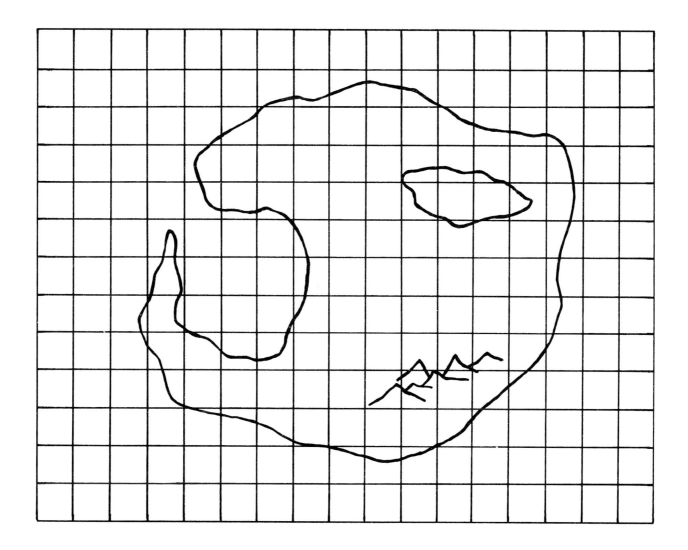

The island

Cut out the plate, knife, fork and spoons and help lay the table.

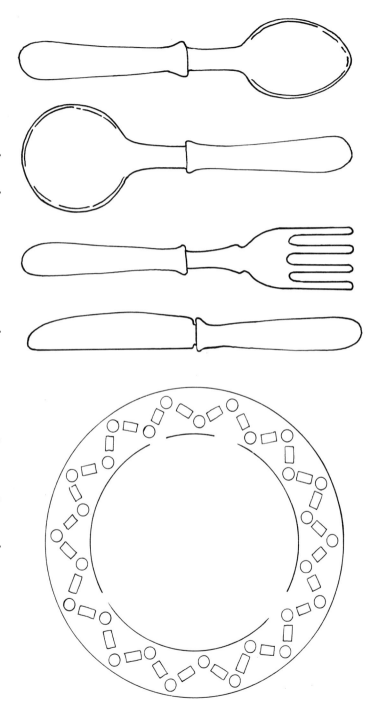

Who is going to buy what?

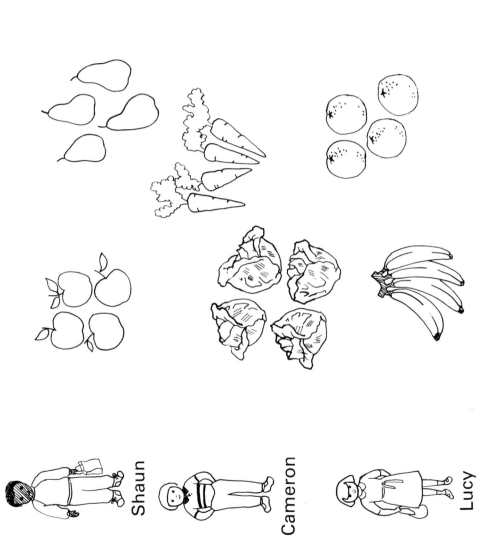

David

Jemma

Rory

Shaun

Cameron

Lucy

This table will give you information about the children.
Look carefully and then answer the questions.

	Favourite Drink	Favourite Snack	Favourite Dinner	Favourite Pudding	Favourite Fruit
Andrew	orange juice	crisps	sausage and chips	yogurt	bananas
Jamie	apple juice	pizza	roast chicken	ice cream	oranges
Mark	milk shake	beans on toast	ham and salad	fruit salad	apples
Amy	cocoa	crisps	cottage pie	ice cream	pears
Your name					

1. Who likes roast chicken best? ———————

2. Who likes ice cream best? ———————

3. Who likes beans on toast best? ———————

4. What is Mark's favourite pudding? ———————

5. What is Andrew's favourite dinner? ———————

6. Which people have the same favourite snack? ———————

7. Who likes pears best? ———————

8. Does Jamie like cocoa best? ———————

9. Does Andrew like fruit salad best? ———————

Here are some examples of food prices. Can you work out the best value product bearing in mind size and price? Some products are "own brand". Does this make a difference?

Number the boxes 1, 2, 3, etc., in order of value for each food.

Coffee

	named brand
100g	£1.39	☐
200g	£2.35	☐

Baked Beans

own brand			named brand		
220g	16p	☐	225g	17p	☐
440g	22p	☐	450g	24p	☐
570g	33p	☐	580g	33p	☐

Cereal

own brand			named brand		
250g	49p	☐	250g	52p	☐
500g	65p	☐	375g	59p	☐
			500g	70p	☐

Tomato Sauce

own brand			named brand		
340g	38p	☐	425g	46p	☐

Frozen Chips

1lb	45p	☐
2lbs	87p	☐
4lbs	£1.39	☐

Peas

8oz	41p	☐
1lb	56p	☐
2lbs	69p	☐
4lbs	£1.20	☐

Write these sums again using numbers and the correct signs.

1. Three add seven. - - - - - - - - - - - -

2. Eight add nine. - - - - - - - - - - - -

3. Twenty-one divided by three. - - - - - - - - - - - -

4. Five multiplied by twenty-five. - - - - - - - - - - - -

5. Three is less than five. - - - - - - - - - - - -

6. Sixteen take away four. - - - - - - - - - - - -

7. Eleven is greater than two. - - - - - - - - - - - -

8. Eighteen minus thirteen. - - - - - - - - - - - -

9. Eight multiplied by three. - - - - - - - - - - - -

10. Find the sum of three and seven. - - - - - - - - - - - -

11. What is the total of twenty and nine? - - - - - - - - - - - -

12. Twenty-two is greater than six add twelve. - - - - - - - - - - - -

13. Thirty-three minus ten equals twenty-seven minus four. - - - - - - - - - - - -

14. Take two pounds fifty from five pounds. - - - - - - - - - - - -

15. Subtract nineteen from thirty-eight. - - - - - - - - - - - -

16. How much longer is one metre than seventy-five centimetres? - - - - - - - - - - - -

17. Share forty-nine apples between seven children. - - - - - - - - - - - -

18. Divide sixty by twelve. - - - - - - - - - - - -

19. Twenty-five times four. - - - - - - - - - - - -

20. Multiply eight by itself. - - - - - - - - - - - -

Give the answer to those questions that need one.

Samuel Morse was an American who invented a telegraphic alphabet, in which letters are represented by combinations of long and short sounds or flashes (dots and dashes).

A .—
B —...
C —.—.
D —..
E .
F ..—.
G ——.
H ....
I ..
J .———
K —.—
L .—..
M ——

N —.
O ———
P .——.
Q ——.—
R .—.
S ...
T —
U ..—
V ...—
W .——
X —..—
Y —.——
Z ——..

Write a message in Morse Code and work out a way of sending it.

Flags that make up the Union Flag ('Union Jack').

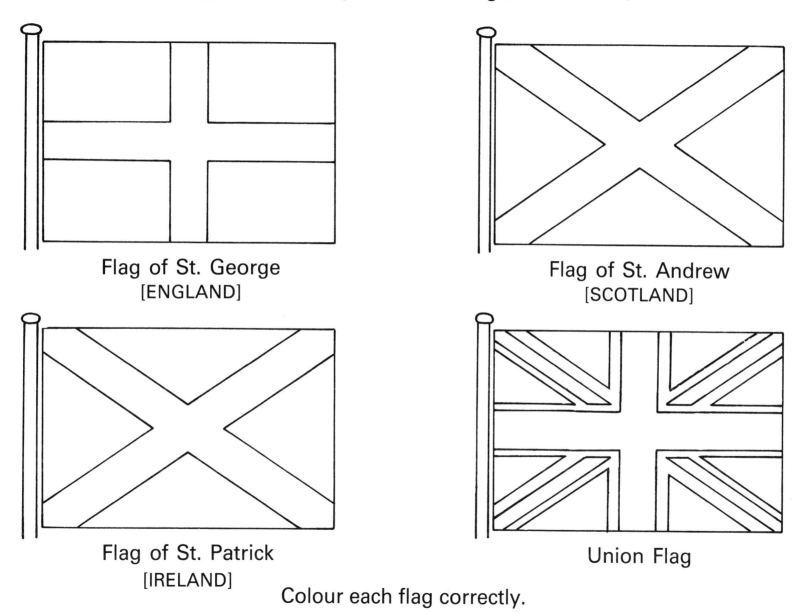

Flag of St. George
[ENGLAND]

Flag of St. Andrew
[SCOTLAND]

Flag of St. Patrick
[IRELAND]

Union Flag

Colour each flag correctly.

SYMBOL SUMS

Find which missing numbers the shapes represent.

	11	14	15	16	
	◯	◁	□	▭	10
	▭	▭	▭	◁	15
	□	⬠	⬠	⬠	16
	▭	◯	⬠	▭	15

3

7

5

6

2

4

1

VERTICAL DISTRIBUTION OF CLOUDS

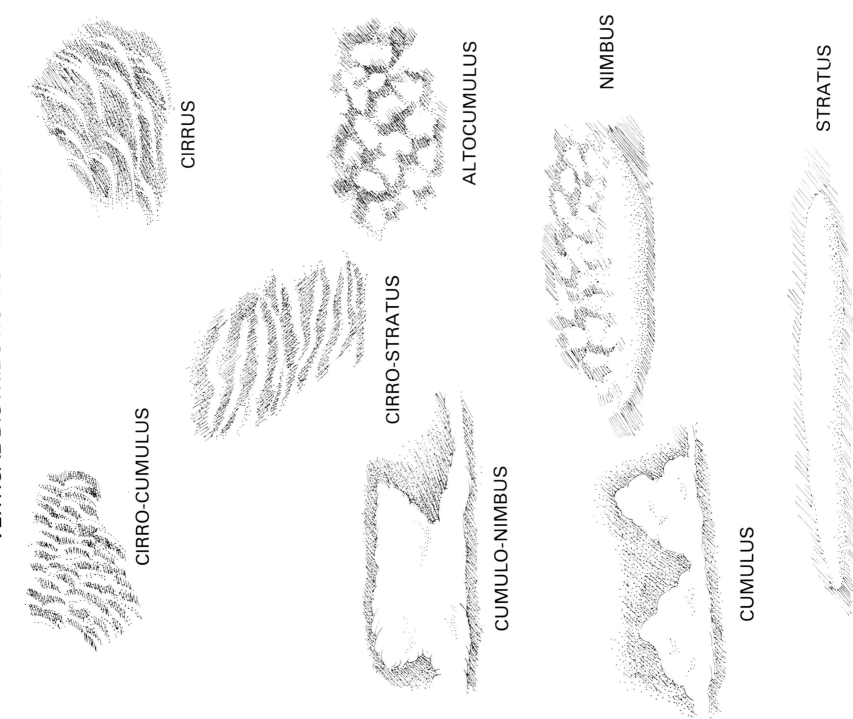

CIRRUS

ALTOCUMULUS

NIMBUS

STRATUS

CIRRO-CUMULUS

CIRRO-STRATUS

CUMULO-NIMBUS

CUMULUS

Some clouds may develop vertically through all levels.

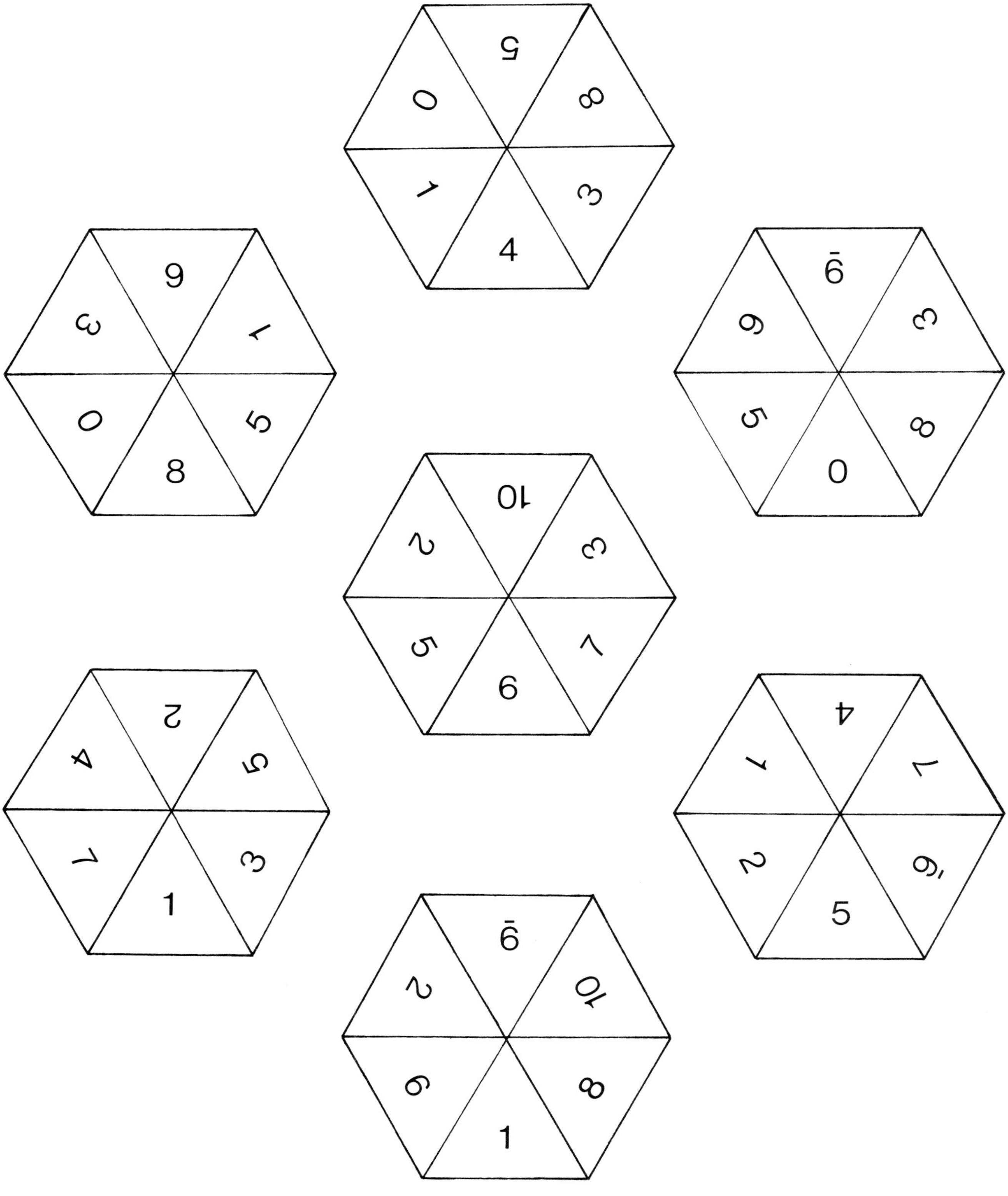

ANGLES

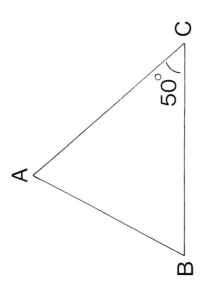

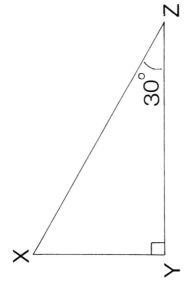

1. Find angle A ----------

2. Find angle B ----------

3. Find angle Y ----------

4. Find angle X ----------

5. Draw a right angle ----------

6. What is an acute angle? ----------

7. What is an obtuse angle? ----------

8. All the angles of a triangle add up to ----------

9. Draw a line AB 6 cm long

   Make angle A = 45° ----------

   Make angle B = 55° ----------

   What size is angle C? ----------

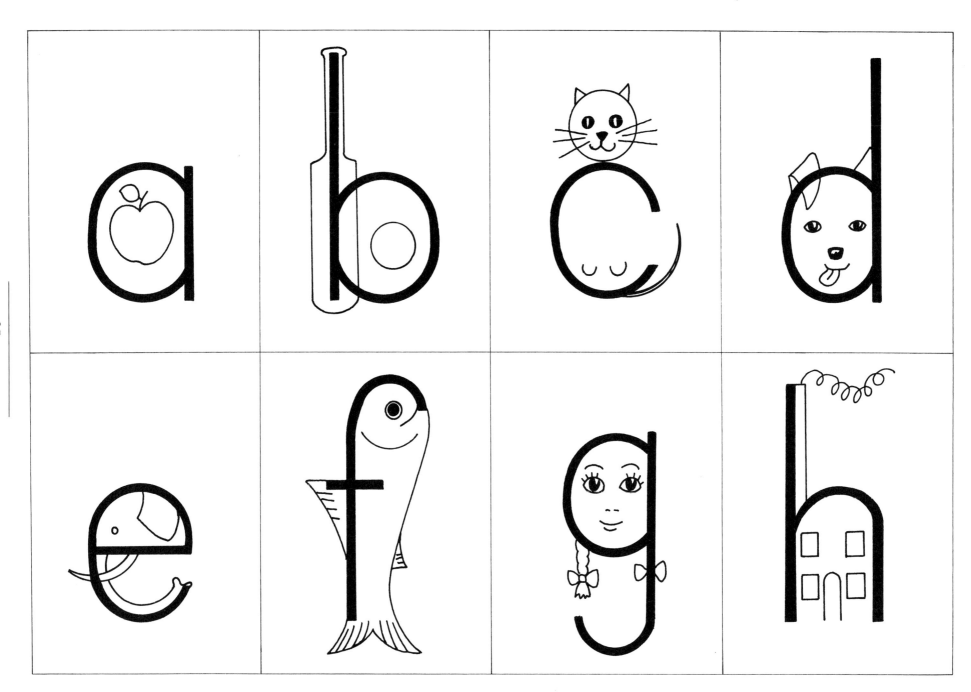

based on
75 Morgan Road
Leicester

Dear John

Are you receiving me This is another space bulletin transmitted by computer on March 9th earth date I hope you are still based with your grandparents while your mum and dad are on holiday Valene and Andrew and I went disco roller skating at our local interplanetary stadium on Saturday Valene is useless and either falls over or crashes into the barrier Andrew and I laugh at her more than anything else I expect you are looking forward to your parents return are they going to bring back a souvenir for you I remember the Boa Constrictor that they brought back from Brazil did you ever find the cat let me know if you can come and stay with us soon

love from
Mark

Can you match the money?

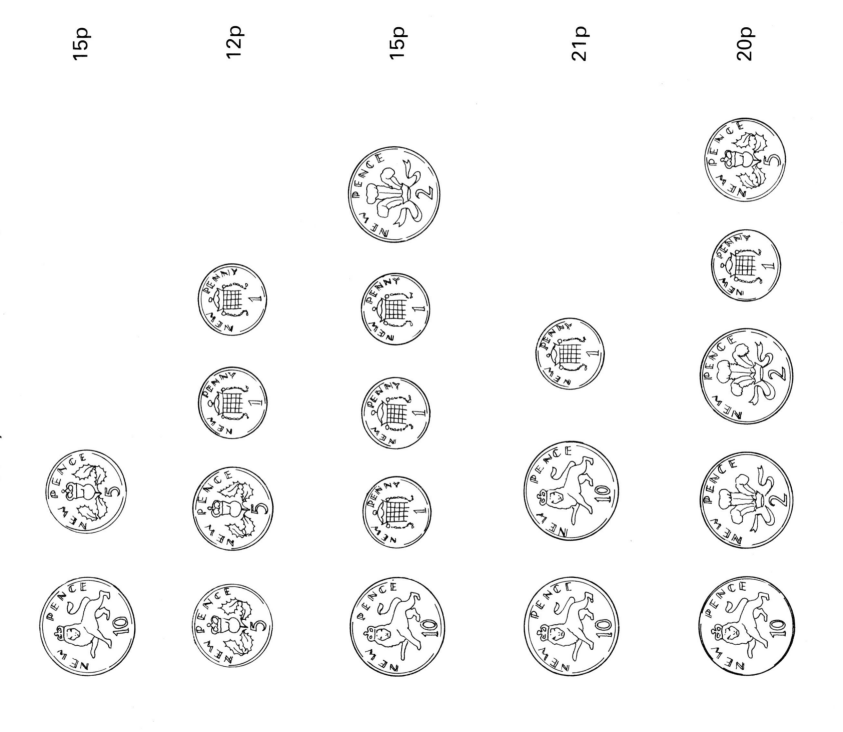

15p

12p

15p

21p

20p

How many ways can you find to make up

10p   5p   6p   14p   8p

© Oliver & Boyd 1986